X

OUR MONEY
OURSELVES

 COUPLES

Also by:
C Diane Ealy, Ph.D., and Kay Lesh, Ph.D.
Our Money, Ourselves: Redesigning Your Relationship with Money

By C Diane Ealy
The Woman's Book of Creativity

Co-authored by Kay Lesh
Building Self-Esteem: Strategies for Success in School and Beyond

OUR MONEY
OURSELVES

for COUPLES

*A New Way of Relating
to Money and Each Other*

C DIANE EALY, PH.D., AND KAY LESH, PH.D.

CAPITAL
BOOKS, INC.

Capital Books, Inc.
P.O. Box 605
Herndon, Virginia 20172-0605

Disclaimer
The names and identifying characteristics of the individuals in this book have been changed in the interest of confidentiality.

The publisher and the authors do not assume, and hereby disclaim, any liability to any party for any loss or damage caused by errors or omissions in *Our Money Ourselves–For Couples.* This book is designed to be a guide, not a replacement for professional counsel, whether therapeutic or financial. It is sold with the understanding that the publisher and the authors are not engaged in rendering therapeutic or financial advice.

Library of Congress Cataloging-in-Publication Data
Ealy, C Diane.
   Our money, ourselves for couples : a new way of relating to money and each other/C Diane Ealy and Kay Lesh.
      p. cm
   Includes index.
   ISBN 1-892123-94-0 (alk. paper)
      1. Finance, Personal—Psychological aspects. 2. Money—Psychological aspects. 3. Married people—Finance, Personal. 4. Unmarried couples—Finance, Personal. I. Lesh, Kay. II. Title.

HG179.E225 2002
332.024'0086'55—dc21

                                                                                         2002017469

Printed in the United States of America on acid-free paper that meets the American National Standards Institute Z39-48 Standard.
First Edition

10   9   8   7   6   5   4   3   2   1

CONTENTS

ACKNOWLEDGMENTS

Every book happens with the support of numerous people. We thank the people who graciously responded to our questionnaire. Our agent, Elizabeth Frost Knappman, was unwavering in her support for this project. We also thank Judy Karpinski, Julie Wrinn, Mary Callahan, and the rest of the staff at Capital Books, Inc. Finally, we are grateful for the love and support of our families, including the cats and dogs.

●INTRODUCTION

We first began working with people on their emotional issues concerning money back in 1990. As therapists and devout observers of human behavior, we had both become aware that a lot of people were increasingly interested in investment possibilities. At the time, the number of individual investors was soaring. But we also saw many people gathering information about what to do with their money to make more money, then failing to follow through with any of this knowledge. Women seemed especially vulnerable to the gather-information-about-money-then-sit-on-it trap. We wanted to find out why. Since both of us were starting private practices at the same time, we were also experiencing our own money issues. Despite our extensive education, no one ever had taught us how to look someone in the eye and ask for a certain amount of money. That act alone brought up a host of deeply buried issues.

Clearly, when people don't have their emotional acts together when it comes to money, they will not implement even the soundest financial advice. We have heard that most readers don't even get through the first quarter of the average financial-planning book before it goes back onto the shelf. When unresolved money issues lurk, they are easily stirred up by any discussion about money. Perhaps this is one of the reasons why discussing money is taboo in the United States.

Along with our research, we began teaching classes in how to redesign one's relationship with money. After each class we consistently felt we had learned at least as much as the people who had attended. Our focus has always been on facilitating the process of identifying beliefs and feelings that contribute to a negative relationship with money, clearing out those barriers, and redesigning, then implementing, a new relationship. We all have a relationship with money in this culture, there's no way around that, although we've been told many times by individuals that they would rather not have anything to do with money. What that means in the majority of cases is that person doesn't want to face his or her emotional issues about money!

So rather than thinking of this experience as a confrontation with some scary, ugly monster with dollar signs dripping all over it, try thinking of it as an opportunity to empower yourself in terms of the currency of this culture. This is a chance for you as an individual, and in tandem with your partner, to design the kind of relationship with money that you want. You can decide what money means and what its purpose is in your life. None of us came into life with a set of beliefs about money—everything in this area has been learned. Now you can sort through the messages and feelings you have acquired about money and decide what to keep and what to toss.

One of the other things that happened while we were teaching classes on money issues is that we both had first books published. Kay co-authored *Building Self-Esteem: Strategies for Success in School* and Diane wrote *The Woman's Book of Creativity*. So one day, probably over lunch, the two of us decided to write a book to help people with their money issues. *Our Money, Ourselves: Redesigning Your Relationship with Money* was released in November 1998. Interestingly, while doing the promotional interviews for that book, we were asked repeatedly about couples and money. We responded by writing this book, designed for opposite-sex, same-sex, and business partners. Regardless of the gender of the people involved, or their purpose in making a commitment to one another, these partnerships require that each person become involved with the other's money issues.

Because this point is so often overlooked, we will repeat that last sentence. When you become involved in a primary or business relationship with another person, you take on that person's issues concerning money. You may be affected in a different way than the other person by those money beliefs, but you will be affected. Having frequent, open discussions with each other about your beliefs and feelings about money is vital to the happy survival of your partnership. This phenomenon is something that ought to be discussed at the very beginning of the relationship, regardless of whether it's personal or business. But this talk seldom takes place.

In this book, we want to provide you with the tools you need to build the kind of relationship you both want with money. In the case of business partners, presumably you are building a business in order to generate income for both of you in a way that meets your individual needs. While making money is not the focus of primary relationships, money difficulties are well known to be one of the principal reasons for the destruction of those partnerships. When the techniques and suggestions in this book are applied on a day-by-day basis, a couple's relationship with money will become clearer, more well-defined, and healthier. Success becomes much more likely under such conditions.

We have divided this book into three parts, basically following the past, present, future timeline. In Part One, "Messages from the Past," we will examine how your past experiences can affect how you interact with money today. We'll look at where your current beliefs came from so that you can begin to acquire a more objective stance in relation to money. In Part Two, "Messages in the Present," we will examine some of the more emotionally charged aspects of money. We will explore topics such as self-worth, emotions, values, secrecy, power, and sex, and look at the ways each ties in with how we relate to money. Finally, in Part Three, "Making Plans," we will guide you in designing and building the relationship you want with money and with each other. After discussing communication, we will suggest ways to write new messages for yourselves, develop a vision, and then realize that vision. We also will make some suggestions regarding the messages you may be giving your children about money. The final chapter focuses on how to continue implementing the changes you both want involving money and its role in your lives.

Thanks for joining us on this wonderful journey. Enjoy!

PART 1

Messages from the Past

1

RECOGNIZING THE ISSUES

The argument had a familiar sound to it. Becky came home from a shopping trip with the girls, ages eleven and fifteen. As usual, they got what they wanted—designer outfits and accessories, along with sports shoes that cost $150 a pair. Andy waited until his daughters were out of earshot before he exploded about the bill, although the look on his face was enough for Becky to know what he was about to say.

"We can't afford to keep running up the charge card. Why do they have to have such expensive things? A blouse is a blouse. It doesn't have to have some guy's name on it to be wearable. And I've seen perfectly good shoes for $40. Besides, they already have nice clothes, and they sure don't need this many more. What were you thinking? Am I the only one who's concerned about our finances? Besides, you know the car needs a brake job and this spring I've got to get a better lawn mower." Even as his last words tumbled out of his mouth, he knew how Becky would react.

"Why do you always pick on me about spending money on the kids? They're only young once, and I want them to have nice things. It's not like I'm spending the money on myself. Do you realize how much you sound like your father?"

"My father has worked hard all his life and he deserves what he has. There's nothing wrong with how he handles money."

"That's not what your mother tells me."

WHAT'S BEHIND THE WORDS

While the content of their arguments about money might vary somewhat, the pattern remains the same for Becky and Andy. She spends money on the children or the house or whatever without consulting him. He gets upset and can always find something else they needed the money for, usually something mechanical. Becky responds by accusing him, one way or the other, of being an insensitive tightwad. Then the argument takes a sharp turn and quickly ends up in left field, astray from the original point. What are they really arguing about? It starts out sounding as if they are upset about money. But we quickly see disagreements about child-rearing, resentments toward in-laws, and perhaps other issues unveiled by their words.

If the argument is solely about money, we can see many different issues. Clearly Becky and Andy do not share a common value system around money and how it ought to be spent. They don't seem to have a shared vision or joint goals. And we might even guess that both are reacting to the situation as a result of their individual experiences with their families as much as they are reacting to each other.

So how do we know when we're arguing about money and when we are really arguing about something else? Usually when couples fight they do so on several levels, so the waters can quickly get muddied. Sometimes they may fight about what's most apparent, the surface issues. Other times they fight about what's below the surface, so the actual issue may stay hidden. For example, suppose my partner agreed to clean up the breakfast dishes before leaving the house, but when I come home I find that the task hasn't been done. When I pick him up at work, I may yell at him for being late and making me sit in the car waiting. While I might be upset about having to wait, my real anger comes from the broken promise about the breakfast dishes. In fact, it's making me angrier than the present situation seems to warrant. This is going to be confusing to my partner, who may decide that I'm overreacting to being kept waiting, especially if he was cornered by his boss at the last minute. I need to be direct about what I'm really angry about and be willing to discuss that issue rather than burying it in another one.

RECOGNIZING THE ISSUES

Recognizing the issues behind a disagreement is critical to effective communication and relationship building. The first step toward this recognition is acknowledging that in many instances when my partner and I disagree about something, many levels are at work. Having done this, we can figure out our next step, which is probably going to be isolating the most important issue and focusing on resolving it. This process is especially important when money is at the center of the disagreement, because so many emotions can get tied up with the issues.

Couples frequently use the dynamic of arguing—about any-thing—to make contact with each other. In other words, they lack adequate physical, emotional, spiritual, or intellectual connection with their partners, and instead of approaching each other from a place of healing, they argue. This at least gives them dynamic contact with each other. Often they follow the fight with "making up," which usually means sex. Couples caught in this web will argue about anything, and attempting to stop the fighting by fixing the apparent problem doesn't work because contact is what they want. They may actually have things in their relationship they disagree about, most couples do. But until they learn how to have loving, meaningful contact with each other, they will not stop fighting. Generally a skilled therapist is required at this point.

Let's assume that Becky and Andy are not this type of couple. How do they know if they are really arguing about money or if other issues are at the core of the problem? More importantly, when you and your partner are having a disagreement that seems to be about money, how do you really know if it's about money or about your relationship—or both? How do you differentiate one issue from an-other?

We suggest both of you ask yourselves some questions about the argument.

Does this argument sound familiar?

Have you had this argument before?

Is there a pattern here?

Did you get off the original point of contention and bring in other issues? (It doesn't matter which one of you did this; the question is, did it happen?)

Did the argument end with one of you giving up?

Did the issues brought up in the argument go unresolved?

In the past have you promised each other not to argue about this topic again, only to have broken that promise now?

If you have argued about this subject in the past, did you give up on trying to resolve it at the time, agreeing to calmly talk later, but never following through?

Does this argument sound familiar to either or both of you because it's similar to arguments your parents had? (Chapters 2 and 3 will help you answer this question.)

Three or more yes answers to these questions means that in all likelihood other issues besides money are behind the argument. Sorting out money issues from other issues is important; it will allow you and your partner to get the most benefit from this book and ultimately build a stronger relationship with each other. As you both delve into your beliefs about money and improve your understanding of your own and your partner's money messages, recognizing the other issues that crop up in money discussions will become easier. But you don't have to be able to do that now in order to benefit from the suggestions described in this book. Clarity will come. Our objective is to turn arguments into discussions, hurt into support and understanding, and unresolved issues into a shared vision with sustaining goals.

SEARCHING BENEATH THE WORDS

Let's take another look at the argument between Becky and Andy. As we break down their words and look at what might be beneath them, think about your own situation and see if you can apply this process to your experiences. We know from Andy's opening sentence, "We can't afford to keep running up the charge card," that the two of them have not agreed on how to use their charge card. If they had such an agreement, then they would be having a discussion about how much could be charged and under what circumstances. He could stop right there and they could discuss money issues.

His next focus is on how Becky used the card, on clothes for their daughters. Now they are really talking about parenting, not money. They apparently don't agree here, either, since Becky seems to believe the girls should get what they want while Andy wants some limits imposed. He's also looking for what he sees as a more reasonable approach to the clothes buying, suggesting that the $40 shoes are just as good as the $150 shoes. Unfortunately for their budget, if they have one, this suggestion won't get discussed because it is surrounded by other issues. Finally, Andy essentially accuses Becky of not caring about their financial situation when he asks "Am I the only one who's concerned about our finances?" He's not looking for an answer to that question, he's venting frustration or anger with a touch of martyrdom thrown in. And his last comment about the brake job and the lawn mower indicates he has his own plans for their money, which he may or may not have discussed with Becky.

We may also get the impression from what Andy has said that the two don't have a budget or at least haven't discussed this particular shopping trip and the budget for it. If this is a familiar argument for this couple—and it sounds as if it is—we get the impression that they do very little talking about basic issues: how to handle money, what are legitimate expenses, how much credit-card debt is acceptable, and what kinds of models they want to create for their daughters regarding money.

Becky's response gives us more insight into just how far apart these two are on actual money issues. We also see the underlying anger. She starts by letting Andy know she feels picked on when he brings up the money she spends on the girls. When she says she wants them to have the best, we might guess that this could come from her own childhood experience. Perhaps her mother always bought her what she wanted while depriving herself. Or Becky's experience might have been the opposite—in other words, she may have had to "settle for second best." So Becky is being a typical parent: treating her children as she was treated—or the exact opposite of how she was treated. Either way, she is in a reactive mode when it comes to spending money on her children.

Becky's next statement is very telling. "It's not like I'm spending the money on myself." Many women have this mindset—that it's okay to buy their children expensive things, even things beyond the budget, but it's not okay to buy themselves nice things. This statement also tells us that in all likelihood these parents have not discussed a budget with their children, nor have they suggested to their daughters that they assume some responsibility for earning money to buy things for themselves.

Then Becky throws Andy a curve when she accuses him of sounding like his father. And he gets distracted. He starts defending his father, which suggests that his wife's accusation probably has some truth to it. As he is defending his father's handling of money, he is also defending his own relationship with money. We tend to repeat behaviors we learned in our families, either by duplicating them or by doing the exact opposite. At this point the argument between Becky and Andy has deteriorated into an argument about Andy's father. Becky's last swipe, "That's not what your mother tells me," lets Andy know that she has an ally in her mother-in-law, and that both women believe there's something wrong with the way Andy and his father handle money. Any hope of resolving the initial point of contention is long gone. Nothing will be resolved; hurt feelings will be buried to rise again another day; the argument will be repeated if not in similar words, certainly in its essence.

STOPPING THE ARGUMENTS

So how do we stop the arguments? Or, for those couples who say they never argue about money but don't talk about it otherwise, how do we get a healthy dialogue started? Hopefully, once you've both gone through this book, the doors to discussion will open and the arguments will stop. In the meantime, remember that it's okay to disagree but how we do it is critical. Couples frequently fall into nonproductive patterns, and breaking free of them takes time and effort from both of you. Be patient with yourselves and each other in this process. Remind yourselves that with practice you will improve your ability to sort out issues. The next couple of chapters in this book will help you look at some of your old patterns and beliefs so you can gain some clarity about your issues while understanding your partner's issues better.

COOLING OFF

Certainly if you find yourself getting into a heated argument, you can say something like, "I'm getting very angry right now and I don't want this to continue. I need to cool off, so I'm going to leave the room, take ten deep breaths, and come back when I can be calm." When tempers are mounting, we suggest that you avoid telling your partner that she or he ought to do the same thing or that she or he is also angry. These words are gasoline on a smoldering fire. Just speak for yourself and get yourself calmed down. Usually a partner who wants to resolve issues rather than perpetuating hurts will do the same thing.

TIMING

When the two of you have something to work out involving money, pick a good time to have the discussion. Don't suddenly bring up an issue as soon as the two of you see each other after work. Allow time for de-stressing from the day and for having positive contact between you. Later in the evening when dinner is finished and chores are completed is probably a better time. If necessary, set up an appointment with each other at a time when you know you won't be interrupted and you will both be rested enough from normal activities to devote your best effort to staying focused and resolving any problems. In other words, set up a money-discussion time that gives you the best chances for success.

CLARIFYING

Before you tackle a money-related issue with your partner, we suggest that you each write down one sentence that summarizes what you think the argument, now a discussion, is really about. Ask yourselves, What is at the core of this issue? Then look at what you each have written. In order to move forward, you must agree on what the conflict is. Often, couples discover that they are each focusing on a different issue. Or that they think the issue is that the other person doesn't handle money the right way. That's shifting blame and condemning, neither of which moves you toward resolution. If you each come up with the same issue, great. If you come up with two different legitimate issues, decide which one you will deal with first. Once that is resolved, move to the second issue or set a time for dealing with it later. Don't sweep it under the rug, or the person who presented that issue will resent its being ignored.

Throughout this book we will provide many activities that you and your partner can do together that will enable you to more clearly understand your own relationship with money, including the family messages you have assimilated and your basic value system as it relates to money. At the same time, you will better understand your partner's beliefs and values. This information can broaden your understanding of what motivates each of you and highlight the underlying reasons for conflicts. With this knowledge you can develop ways to work together to strengthen your relationship with each other as you strengthen your relationship with money.

AN ACTIVITY

Many of the activities we have designed ask you and your partner to first complete a written list or questionaire without discussion, and then share your responses with each other. In this way, you will gain more insight into how the other thinks and feels about the issue at hand. At the same time, writing about the issue will help diffuse the emotion around it that often clouds and sidetracks an effort to talk. Each of you might want to have a special "money journal" to use as you work your way through this book. It helps to keep everything related to your money discussions in one place and serves as a reminder of what you have accomplished.

Let's start this process with each of you writing down what you think are your most frequently discussed or argued-about issue(s) concerning money. Give yourselves several minutes to write. The next step is to read them to each other. To determine if there are hidden issues underlying the ones you've written down, subject each one to the questions on pages 5–6. Often another person's perspective on an issue can give us insight that we can't come up with by ourselves.

Practice speaking from your own experience and concerns instead of focusing on what you think your partner is doing. For example, Andy's communication would have been much more effective if, instead of saying, "We can't afford to keep running up the charge card," he had said, "I get really worried when I think our debts are getting out of control." Becky might not have felt under attack and may have been more willing to listen if he had taken that approach. In that situation she might have been able to keep cool and avoid getting into the old argument pattern.

As you identify issues, practice owning them by using "I" statements rather than "you" statements. Sentences like "I worry that . . . ," "I want us to . . . ," and "I get angry when . . ." serve to open communication. Phrases like "When you . . . ," "You always . . . ," and "You never . . ." are guaranteed to close off discussion. Who feels like discussing issues when they see themselves as being under attack?

If you have both written down the same issues, great. You're on the same wavelength. If you have identified different issues, avoid the trap of having to defend what you've written. When something is an issue for one of you, it's an issue for both. Seeing different areas of concern regarding money just means you have variations in your value systems—what's important to you may not be as important to your partner. That's okay as long as you are both willing to accept the other's viewpoint.

You don't have to attempt to resolve these issues right now. You've probably had them hanging around for quite a while, so a little longer won't hurt. Opening the door to understanding is what's important at this point. As you move through this book, you will learn techniques to resolve them while building a clearer relationship with money.

SOME WORDS OF ENCOURAGEMENT

Take some time to appreciate your own and your partner's courage in discussing these tough topics. Most couples find money issues to be loaded with emotion and confusion. The very fact that you've made a start in talking about money as a couples issue speaks to your willingness to work together to make some changes. Good for you! The task is indeed challenging, and you will probably experience some temporary discomfort. We predict you will find that the rewards make the struggle worthwhile.

MOVING FORWARD ▶▶▶▶▶▶▶▶▶

Our objective in this chapter is to provide a solid foundation for helping you and your partner turn arguments into discussions, hurt into support and understanding, and unresolved issues into a shared vision with sustainable goals. As each of you practices the steps we have summarized below, you will move toward building an improved relationship with each other and with money.

1. Begin unraveling your issues concerning money by acknowledging the multiple emotions involved.

2. Shift your mindset from having arguments about money to having discussions.

3. Pick a good time for both of you to discuss money issues.

4. Clarify the discussion by writing down in one sentence what you think it is about.

5. Keep a money journal to track issues clarified, communication successes, and other elements of your progress as you move through this book.

6. Work through the activity described at the end of this chapter. Isolate an issue, subject it to the questions under "Recognizing the Issues," practice using "I" statements, allow yourself to see your partner's perspective.

7. Take a break from the discussion if you begin to get angry.

2

THE QUESTIONNAIRE

Inspiration for this book has come from the workshops and individual sessions we have conducted to help people redesign their relationship with money and with their partners. Once individuals overcome their initial reluctance to discuss money, feelings and opinions flow. We are always fascinated by what the couples in our groups have to say about the role money plays in their lives and their relationships. Such topics as learning about money in their families as they grew up, deciding how to divide up the couple's financial responsibilities and tasks, and even the battles they have had over money all sparked lively discussions. Shared information, insights, and observations from couples have given shape and direction to our work. As you work through this book, you will gain insight and probably even feel a measure of camaraderie as you read about our participants and what they have been willing to bring to this endeavor.

Our face-to-face contact with couples has been invaluable. As we noted what they had to say, we found ourselves excited by new ideas and possibilities. Couples have brought up issues and feelings we knew would resonate with just about anyone involved in a relationship. We wanted to know more. The input we had received was so useful that we were anxious to tap into the wisdom of as many couples as we could. We designed a questionnaire so that we could reach even more people, and we expanded our definition of "couple" to include any two people in a relationship where money is an important aspect. Marriage obviously fits this definition, but so does two people in a committed, primary relationship. Business partners certainly take on each other's approaches to and concerns about money, so they are also included.

PUTTING THOUGHTS TO PAPER

Most couples found the questionnaire took some time and effort and a few couples never finished filling it out. "Too painful," "Too difficult," "This brings up too many issues that we aren't ready to deal with," were responses we got from those who were unable to complete it. Some women told us that while they had answered the questions, their husbands hadn't. The women always seemed surprised by this. We knew from our experience with *Our Money, Ourselves: Redesigning Your Relationship with Money* that some people are just not ready to deal with their money issues. We respect that. And we applaud the self-awareness that couples demonstrate by telling us they are not yet up to the task of tackling such a thorny issue.

The majority of couples we asked did complete our questionnaire. By doing so, they received an unexpected bonus—the questionnaire intended to help us write a book turned out to be equally helpful to the respondents. Feedback from the couples we surveyed told us that the process of responding to this questionnaire on money issues was both powerful and thought-provoking.

Putting thoughts to paper is a powerful process. Many of us have experienced flashes of insight and clarity from jotting down our ideas in a journal. Couples reported a similar experience. They found that filling out the questionnaire took thought and soul-searching, helping them in several ways. Answering our questions provided them with the opportunity to clarify some of their own issues. More importantly, they gained insight into the ideas and beliefs of their partners when they shared their responses with each other. Many lightbulbs were turned on. Because the couples had their completed questionnaires in front of them when they talked, they found it easier to keep away from the emotional baggage so often attached to money and to stay focused on the financial issues themselves.

AN INVITATION TO PARTICIPATE

We invite you to do the same. Our hope is that you, like other couples, will find our questionnaire valuable in identifying core beliefs, issues, potential conflicts, and areas of agreement. These can serve as a guide as you work with your partner on resolving joint and individual money issues. With these benefits in mind, we have reproduced the questionnaire we used in our survey below.

We suggest you and your partner each fill out separate questionnaires without consulting each other as you do so. You can share responses later, but initially it is important to capture your own thoughts without any input from anyone else. Once you have written everything you have to say, put the questionnaire away for a little while and just allow your unconscious mind to work on it. When you look at your answers after this resting period, new ideas may come to you. Be sure to add whatever insights you gain, without censoring yourself.

Our Money, Ourselves—For Couples Questionnaire

1. What messages did you get as a child around money and earning money?

2. How have these messages influenced you as an adult?

3. Please complete the following sentences in two different ways: first as you would; next as you believe your partner would.

(self) Money is _____

(partner) Money is _____

(self) When I think about my relationship with money, I recognize that _____
_____

(partner) When I think about my relationship with money, I recognize that _____
_____

(self) Security is _____

(partner) Security is _____

4. How much did you and your partner discuss your attitudes toward money prior to living together?

5. What kind of discussions did you and your partner have about individual incomes and credit histories before living together?

6. What common money goals do you and your partner have?

7. Do you and your partner have combined or separate:

    Checking   Savings   Investments

8. How often do you and your partner argue about money:

    Often   Sometimes   Rarely   Never

9. What issues do you usually argue about?

10. How are these arguments resolved?

11. What would you would like to change in how you and your partner relate to money?

12. The biggest difference I see between my partner and me concerning money is _____

SHARING YOUR QUESTIONNAIRES

When your work on the questionnaire feels finished, you are ready to compare answers with your partner. Look for areas of agreement and disagreement. How similar are your answers? How do they differ? What surprises you? What did you already know? Jot your answers in your money journal, noting topics you and your partner need to work on. Remember to focus on only one issue at a time, sticking with that one until it is resolved.

The questionnaire is an important first step in exploring your money messages. We hope it piqued your curiosity about what else lies ahead. We invite you to continue your journey of discovery.

MOVING FORWARD ▶▶ ▶▶ ▶▶ ▶▶ ▶▶ ▶

The questionnaire is a starting point in discussing money issues with your partner. Responding to the questions will give you an idea of points in your relationship where money conflicts are likely to occur. You can also begin to pinpoint some of the areas needing further work. As you progress through this book, you will hone in on the money issues of major importance to you, and more in-depth discussions will be possible. For now, your goal is to develop some general sense of what money means to you based on messages from your family.

Be aware that writing down your responses to the questionnaire might stir up some emotions. If that's the case, you are not alone. Money is an emotional issue for many of us. Our goal is to take the emotion out of it so that you can look at your conflicts from a cool-headed viewpoint and make some needed changes.

Here are some steps for you to follow for now:

1. List some of the family money messages you have identified. Briefly note how you believe these messages have influenced you as an adult.

2. Think about the last money fight you had with your partner. If you had to summarize the issue in one sentence, what would you say?

3. List the areas of money conflict with your partner. What patterns do you see?

4. Write a paragraph describing an ideal relationship with your partner. How does money fit into your relationship?

3

EXPLORING YOUR
MONEY ATTITUDES

"I don't know why I reacted that way. I just did!" Sound familiar? We've all made this statement and we've certainly heard others make it as well. From the sound of it, we might suppose that our behavior just happens. Human beings do seem to behave in mysterious ways, and sometimes our own behavior is the most mystifying. But rarely is behavior as mystifying as it seems. Usually with some effort, we can identify the reasons why we do what we do.

Without really being aware of it, we act on what we have learned in the past. Thus, we are likely to respond to situations in predictable ways based on what has gone before. Because these responses usually are not part of our conscious thought, they can be confusing, complex, and occasionally surprising. Bringing these responses to the level of consciousness lessens our confusion. With this awareness we can decide if they serve us well. If what we are doing is working for us, great. For most of us, however, our old automatic responses reflect who we were in the past, not who we are today. Many of our old messages need to be evaluated and possibly retooled and revised to fit us in the present and serve us in the future. This is especially true of our money messages.

EVALUATING OLD MESSAGES

The need to evaluate old messages becomes especially urgent when we find ourselves in an intimate relationship. Not only are we affected by our own messages, but we also must contend with the messages the other person brings to the relationship. Taking some time to understand the messages that direct our and our partner's behaviors can keep us from repeating nonproductive and even unhealthy behavior patterns.

To understand our behavior in a relationship, we need to view our individual messages, especially the ones we learned in our early years, since they tend to be deeply embedded in the psyche. Keep in mind that we gather information in two ways—directly and indirectly. Understanding both types of messages will help us understand our present behaviors. Let's look at direct messages first.

Direct Messages

As we grow up we are constantly bombarded with lessons and instructions. We learn to read, write, and do our sums as a result of what happens in a classroom. Advertisers tell us what to buy. Parents and other significant adults give us information to keep us well behaved, civilized, and safe. "Don't speak to strangers" and "Don't spend all your money on candy" are clear directives of what not to do. "Say thank you for Grandma's gift" and "Save for a rainy day" let us know what we should do. Heard in childhood, such clear and powerful messages remain with us into adulthood, becoming part of our belief system and guiding our behavior. Do we still need to be cautioned: "Take your elbows off the table when you eat"? Very rarely—we just do it automatically. Even when we think we have discarded these direct messages, they are often still with us. The very fact that people put so much effort into *not* being like their parents demonstrates the hold of this type of early learning. Whether we agree or disagree with our early messages, their pull is strong indeed.

Identifying Direct Messages   The following activity will help you begin to identify some of the direct messages you may have received in the past. We suggest that both partners do this activity separately before discussing it. Concentrate on your own answers, taking all the time you need to give thoughtful responses to the questions. We encourage you to write the answers to the following questions in your money journal.

How would your mother describe her family role regarding money?

How would your father describe his family role regarding money?

Who made the money decisions in the family? Were decisions made cooperatively or unilaterally? How do you know this?

Was one parent a spendthrift and the other a tightwad? Who took each role? How was this difference in views dealt with?

Did your parents fight about money? Was there an ongoing theme to the fights? Whose side did you take? How were these fights resolved?

What spiritual or religious messages did you receive about money?

What was the prevailing view of money in your school and neighborhood?

What ethnic/cultural messages did you receive about money?

What other direct messages about money did you receive?

Now you've begun to tap into your direct messages about money. Additional messages are bound to occur to you as you progress through this book. Take the time to write them down so you can refer to them later. Trade your list of direct messages with your partner so you can compare their similarities and differences. When reading your partner's responses and discussing differences, remember to avoid judging. Your goal here is to increase your mutual understanding of each other's money beliefs. Neither of you is right, neither is wrong. Keeping this in mind relieves some of the tension inherent in exploring this topic, so you can just focus on learning more about yourself and your partner.

Indirect Messages

By observing others in our family and community and by participating in the rituals of our families, we have also learned indirect lessons throughout our lives. We absorbed the attitudes, beliefs, and emotions of those around us and then drew conclusions about how the world worked based on what we believed we saw. For example, if we watched the women in our families devote their lives to being stay-at-home moms, we learned that this is how women behave. Watching the men in our families work two jobs to send children to a private, religious school gave us another message about the value of religion as well as how responsibility should be demonstrated. This kind of learning is extremely powerful because we internalize it without question and it thus becomes a part of us.

Most people are surprised to learn just how many of our money messages fall into this indirect learning category. We can usually remember most of our direct messages. But the majority of messages that dictate how we should think, feel, and behave in relation to money are acquired indirectly. We observe the important people in our lives and draw conclusions based on what we see. These kinds of messages are more challenging to talk about because they tend to be deeply buried in the psyche.

The Power of Early Messages   Here is an example of how our early messages work. Notice that we either accept or reject them. Rarely do we totally ignore them.

> Patty and Clark make a couples ritual out of paying the bills. They set aside time at the beginning of each month and write all the checks for the mortgage, utilities, and other household expenses. After a brief discussion, they decide how much to allow for discretionary spending and how much to save. "This is how my parents handled money," says Patty. "They always sat down together and worked their finances this way. Clark and I thought it was a great way to deal with expenses and have followed this pattern since our marriage three years ago. It works for us."
>
> Margaret and Frank have a similar ritual. Like Patty and Clark, they find a mutually convenient time to pay their bills and make financial decisions. Working cooperatively helps them feel like a team, they report. Although both couples follow a similar ritual, their reasons for doing so are completely opposite. "Growing up, I saw my mother totally left out of the financial loop," says Margaret. "Dad paid the bills and gave Mom a household allowance. She knew nothing about what was going on and had no say in decision-making. I thought it was really demeaning and I vowed

not to operate like that in my marriage. That's why we devised this plan where we can share in the work and the decision process."

THE GENOGRAM

We all carry messages from the past that guide our behavior even though we may not be consciously aware of their impact. A powerful method of bringing family messages to a conscious level is a type of psychological family tree called a genogram. When we construct a genogram, we are able to see family patterns in a clear and graphic way, while avoiding the temptation to blame. These old patterns are especially important for couples to identify. What we know about how people "should" behave in a relationship was learned in our family, so each partner brings these strong messages into a relationship. Because we are not always consciously aware of the information we carry, we cannot share it with our partner. We just act and react, and the mystery of our behavior deepens. Understanding these patterns demystifies our actions, weakens the messages, and gives us the opportunity to evaluate and rewrite messages that no longer work.

Examining and discussing our family money messages using a genogram also helps to diffuse much of the emotion clinging to the messages. This is a critical step in discussing money issues with each other. Defensiveness, fear, anger, and similar emotions can quickly enshroud issues, diverting our attention as we sink from discussion into argument. Having your genograms in front of you helps keep the discussion objective.

Constructing Your Own Genogram

Here's how to construct a genogram so you can identify your own messages and see family patterns. You will gain a wealth of information from this activity, making the time you spend in doing your genogram a smart investment. We suggest that you and your partner construct your genograms independently, sharing them only when you're finished.

Gather together marking pens or crayons and several large sheets of drawing paper or smaller sheets of typing paper you can later tape together. Allow a minimum of 20 minutes to work. You may choose to complete your genogram in several sessions to allow enough thinking time. Have plenty of space to spread your work out—you'll need it!

Genograms utilize certain symbols for clarity and consistency. They are:

a square designates male:

a circle, female:

the symbol for marriage is:

divorce is:

children are shown as:

a death is:

1982

Fred 1981   Mary 1984

closeness between family members is

distance is:

Once you've got the right supplies and know the basic symbols, sit back, relax and spend some time just thinking about your family. Some people find that looking through old family photos helps to put them in the right mindset. Visualize yourself and the preceding generations. Begin the genogram by drawing your generation: you, your siblings, and everyone's mates. Include divorces, deaths, still-born children, abortions, and as much information as you can remember. Once you get started, you will probably find you remember much more than you expected to.

Here's an example:

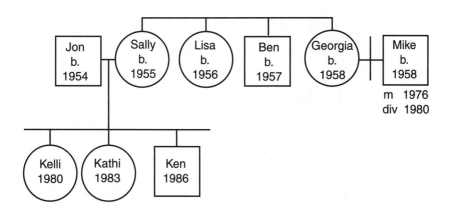

Next work back to your mother's generation and sketch out her family. Again, be sure to include siblings and their mates and children as you did for your own generation. Add the same information for your father's family.

Now you are ready for your grandparents and their families. Do the same with them, again including as much information as you can remember. If you are a parent of grown children, you will probably wish to include them as well, making a four-generation genogram. You will no doubt see patterns emerge as children follow their understanding of family messages.

Looking at Family Patterns

Once you have the basic information, you can fill in more of your genogram using the following suggestions. As you do this, continue to be aware of patterns.

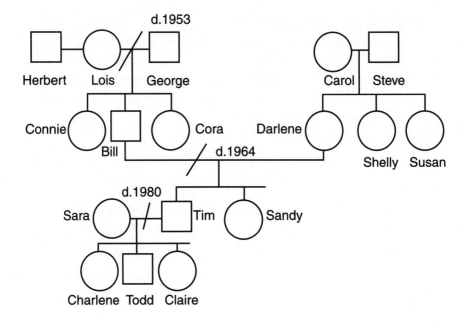

- List the education level and employment of family members.

- Make a guess at the income level of family members. You may not know exact details, but at least classify each nuclear family as lower-, middle-, or upper-class.

- Jot down the ages at which people in your family married. Note divorces and the reasons, if you know them. Add in any extramarital liaisons, out-of-wedlock children, and other pieces of information related to marriage. These pieces all have an impact on money.

- Note the kind of partners the people in your family chose. You may notice a pattern of partners who were chronically underemployed or who couldn't hold a job. Or you may see the opposite—partners who were workaholics. Again, list as much information as you can about common marital patterns.

- Which family members stand out for either lower or higher income? Did anyone break a family pattern? What did they do? How did other family members regard them?

- List the predominant family patterns you see. Be especially aware of any gender patterns.

- Note patterns of closeness and distance. Did choice of partners influence the closeness or distance of family members? How was family loyalty demonstrated? Disloyalty?

- Return to the questionnaire in Chapter 2. Reread it to see if any additional patterns emerge. Also review your answers in the Identifying Direct Messages Activity on pages 20 and 21 to see if they jog any memories.

- If you were to compose a family motto regarding money, what would it be? Write it beside your genogram.

- Do you see any repeated money conflict patterns for the couples in your family? List them.

- Finally, list anything else about your family that provides information about your current money issues with your partner.

The genogram is a powerful tool for raising awareness about a couple's conflicts and concerns. As you look at yours, be aware of all the messages that it evokes. When you share your genogram with your partner, you may become aware of other insights as you discuss family messages. Be sure to record these in your money journal.

Processing Genograms With Your Partner
As with all the activities throughout this book, your goal in creating a genogram is sharing information with your partner. You'll want to be especially conscious of the emotional impact money messages can have so you can be encouraging and respectful of your own and your partner's disclosures. We encourage you both to be cautious about giving unsolicited feedback. Your insights may be brilliant and on target, but if your partner is not ready to hear them you both could end up with hurt feelings. Be sure to ask permission before offering opinions or insights. And be sure to say "no" if you're not ready to hear your partner's feedback at that time.

Questions to Consider   The following questions are intended to help spark discussion with your partner as you discuss your genogram.

You needn't be limited by our suggestions. Feel free to add questions of your own.

What money messages do we share? How do our messages differ?

What were the gender roles involving money in our families? Who was in charge of finances? Who was in charge of making the money? Are these roles repeating in our relationship?

What money battles were fought in our families? Are they being repeated in our current relationship?

What similarities or differences do you see in mate selection in each of our families?

How does this affect our attitudes about money?

Compare family money mottoes. Are they similar? How do they differ?

What else do we notice about our family messages?

ONE COUPLE'S FAMILY MESSAGES

As you both work through your genograms and share insights with each other, you can see the hold indirect messages have over us. We act in accordance with these messages in relationships without giving them much conscious thought, because the behavior is familiar to us. Once we bring our messages to a conscious level, we gain the power to decide whether they still fit for us. When messages no longer fit, it's time to make a change. Here's an example of how this dynamic can work.

Many of Fred and Berna's money arguments involved buying groceries. Berna, a gourmet cook, was always on the lookout for new and different foods to spark her creative efforts. She would buy exotic ingredients to try and had no qualms about tossing something down the garbage disposal if the results weren't up to her standards. Fred cringed each time something was thrown out, accusing Berna of waste and needless extravagance. Berna's standard response was that if Fred could buy every tool in the hardware store, she could have fun with her hobby, cooking, and he should be glad she was so creative.

When they shared their genograms, Berna and Fred found several important differences in their respective money messages. Fred came from a very frugal family whose motto, "Waste not, want not," was still driving him today. The son of a father who was frequently out of work, Fred had learned to make things last as long as possible and to never, never be extravagant. It was okay, however, to buy things like tools. In his family, tools were viewed as functional—they lasted and could be used to repair things, further extending the useful life of household items. Food was considered utilitarian—the family was more concerned with how far basic staples could be stretched rather than with how many fancy things could be done with them. Spending money on anything that was not absolutely necessary just didn't happen in Fred's family. It was hard enough to make the budget cover daily needs. Buying anything beyond basics was considered reckless spending.

Berna's family was comfortable financially. Their motto was "Money is to help you enjoy life, so have fun with it." Berna had never really given much thought to her attitude toward spending. She was still acting on her family message and was unconcerned about the cost of anything she really wanted. In Berna's world, food was a creative adventure—there was always plenty, so why not enjoy it? Besides, it was fun to experiment and come up with new dishes.

As Fred and Berna talked about their genograms, they were able to see that their conflicting messages were getting them into trouble needlessly. His message, "Be careful with money," directly contradicted her message, "Money is to enjoy." They valued their relationship and really wanted to stop the fighting. As they discussed their family messages, they recognized that they both were acting on old directives rather than the current reality: they weren't wealthy but they were comfortable financially.

Coming up with a grocery-shopping strategy that worked for them both involved discussing goals and making some compromises. Fred became less ready to label Berna's purchases as "extravagances" and was able to relax a bit so he could enjoy her culinary creativity. Berna became more conscientious about staying within the reasonable food budget they had established. She also acknowledged that she really valued his ability to fix things around the house, even though she didn't see the necessity for all of his tool purchases. As they learned to allow more give and take when it came to money issues, they became more appreciative of each other's strengths. They created new money messages that were a reflection of their current lives instead of their parents' realities.

MOVING FORWARD ▶ ▶ ▶ ▶ ▶ ▶ ▶ ▷

Identifying your early money messages is an important step in developing a new experience with money. By understanding the impact of the past, you can deal more effectively with the present. You have given yourself the power to choose messages that fit your situation today, basing your decisions on current reality, not the habits of the past. As you and your partner begin making conscious choices based on the insights you have developed, you will find that your relationship becomes stronger and more honest.

Here are some things you can do to help you identify old messages. You will want to do your individual work before you and your partner share insights.

1. Go back to the section on direct messages in this chapter and answer the questions regarding your family money messages.

2. Construct your own genogram, following the directions above. Take your time and gather as much information as you can.

3. Make a list of your direct and indirect money messages. Using a colored highlighter, mark the ones that strike you as most important.

4. Select a mutually convenient time to share your money messages with your partner. Choose a time when you both are ready to listen and learn from each other.

5. Using the list you have developed, discuss your direct and indirect messages with your partner, in a supportive, nonjudgmental atmosphere.

6. Identify the messages you each bring to the relationship. Which ones are complementary? Which ones are likely to cause problems?

7. Decide which messages you want to keep, which ones need to be revised, and which ones need to be discarded?

8. Write the new money messages you want to incorporate into your lives. Be willing to continue to work with your partner until you both are comfortable with the new messages you have devised. Commit to additional sessions if it seems appropriate.

9. Plan a celebration to commemorate the inauguration of your new family messages and to give yourselves a reward for a job well done.

CULTURAL MESSAGES

The terrifying plunge into the icy waters of the North Atlantic had left Jack and Rose physically and emotionally battered. Now as they struggled through the wreckage of what had been the once mighty *Titanic,* the anguished cries of their fellow passengers filled the night. The dead and dying surrounded them. As the waves crashed and tore the strength from their bodies, Jack heroically boosted Rose to safety aboard a chunk of floating debris. Since there was only room for her, he clung to the side of the makeshift raft. With all the energy he had left, Jack exhorted Rose to live her life fearlessly and let nothing stop her from achieving her dreams. She promised to do so, then fell into an exhausted stupor. Rose awoke in time to see Jack's frozen body slipping into the icy depths. Even their love could not save him.

As we watched the blockbuster film *Titanic,* some of the less romantic among us have wondered why Jack didn't use his remaining strength to swim to a similar piece of wreckage so he too could be saved. Or why Rose didn't remind him to find his own raft. But of course doing so would certainly have diminished the drama of the movie, to say nothing of leaving Rose without any inspiration for living the rest of her life. And such action would have gone counter to some important cultural messages firmly embraced by Rose and Jack. He took the role of rescuer; she was the one to be rescued. Rose and Jack were only doing what their culture said they should do—they were playing out their assigned roles.

PLAYING OUT OUR CULTURAL ROLES

Like Jack and Rose, we too follow directives from our culture. These messages reflect our culture's view of how things "ought" to be and shape the roles we are expected to play. We feel the impact of these views in all aspects of our relationships, especially in our dealings with money. Our actions in relation to money—as we earn it, save it, share it, spend it—demonstrate our interpretation of these directives.

You know from the previous chapter that family messages have a major influence in shaping our dealings with money. By now, you can identify many of your own family money messages and are aware of their effect on you. As important as these messages are in helping us understand our money behaviors, they don't provide a total explanation. That is because our family messages don't occur in a vacuum. They are shaped and influenced by the culture in which we live. As these two powerful forces, family and culture, interact, they determine how we are likely to behave as males and females, how we see ourselves in relationships, and especially how we relate to money. So to fully understand our money behaviors we need to take a look at our cultural directives. Where do they come from and what do they tell us? And what do we do with this information? Do we act in concert with our messages or do we push against them? The answers to these questions will give you more insights and information that will be useful as you work with your partner to enhance your relationship.

HOW CULTURAL DIRECTIVES SHAPE OUR MONEY BEHAVIORS

Our culture shapes our lives and behaviors. The expectations our culture has for us affect our money behaviors in ways that sometimes surprise us. Cultural directives, especially those having to do with money in relationships, aren't always clearly stated. Much of the time, they are just a part of our lives, and we absorb them because we live them, accepting them without much thought. They become a part of us. Much of the time we aren't consciously aware of our cultural directives until an unexamined notion of how things should be conflicts with what is. Let's see how this might be played out in one couple's relationship.

Margo and Peter love each other. In spite of this, however, they are having ongoing battles over money. The fights have escalated in recent months, becoming more and more bitter. The couple has reached the point where they both question whether they want to continue their relationship. This fighting is new for them. There was a time when they could work together, set common goals, and act cooperatively. Something changed.

Margo and Peter met at the State University and married when they were at the halfway point in their graduate-school programs. Peter's easygoing manner and his concern for the well-being of others were qualities that Margo, a business major, found very attractive. She thought his profession of choice, social work, was perfect for him. "He is the kind of person who can really make a difference in the world," she frequently told her friends. Peter, in turn, appreciated Margo's computer wizardry and applauded her decision to become a computer analyst.

When they married, they were both self-supporting, getting by on part-time work, student loans, and grants. They were accustomed to the starving student role and accepted the limitations the college lifestyle placed on them. As a couple, they happily cooperated, pinching pennies, clipping coupons, and saving so they could meet their tuition payments as well as household expenses. "Cutting corners today means a better future for us in the long run," they reminded each other when they postponed buying some desired treat. They were committed to graduate work in their respective programs and were supportive of each other both emotionally and financially. It seemed they faced a bright future together.

When that future finally arrived, Margo and Peter were surprised by the problems that cropped up. Instead of enjoying their new financial freedom as they had expected, they found themselves fighting more about money than they ever did during their penny-pinching graduate school days. Their spirit of cooperation had evaporated, replaced by constant arguments over how much they could afford to spend. Their very different views about how they should deal with spending led to constant bickering.

"I'm ready to have some classy furniture after the thrift-store stuff we had in grad school," Margo told us, describing a huge fight she and Peter recently had. "I ordered a gorgeous leather sofa that I found on sale at a great price. I thought Peter would be thrilled. I knew he was as anxious as I to get rid of the junk-store bargains we had in our apartment. When the dream sofa was delivered, Peter just hit the roof. He became totally irrational. He says he can't pay his half of it, so we can't afford it. I say who cares? I make enough money to easily afford this great sofa. What's the big deal here? I never thought we'd be fighting like this over such stupid stuff."

"It's a big deal to me," Peter angrily responded. "I didn't think it would matter, but I really hate the fact that you make more money than I do. I can't afford that sofa on my salary and that's that! It goes back and we'll wait until I can afford to pay my share."

What's going on here? How did a couple, previously functioning in such harmony about shared goals, end up in angry battles? They still love each other devotedly, but something is getting in the way. Because of the fields they have chosen, Margo and Peter are faced with large differences in take-home pay. Margo, who took a computer-consultant job with a large firm, brings home almost twice as much money as Peter does. Peter loves his job as a school social worker. He is committed to working with youth, and it feels good to him to be making a difference in their lives. At the same time, he finds himself irritable and nitpicking with Margo over money issues. "I never dreamed that this could be such a big deal to me," Peter said. "I am surprised at how much it bothers me that she makes more money than I do. I guess it makes me feel like less of a man, even though I know that isn't logical. I keep thinking of my father and what he would say about a man's duties to his family."

THE HAZARDS OF IGNORING OUR MESSAGES

Peter's discomfort at earning less than his wife churned up all sorts of feelings that he never knew he had. Like most of us, Peter never really needed to examine the messages he was carrying with him. These cultural directives and the roles that accompany them are so much a part of us that we usually are aware of them only when we go against them. Then we get a jolt that quickly lets us know that we are going against a deeply held yet unexamined belief about how things should be.

Peter's strong emotional reaction to earning less money than his wife is an example of how this jolt can be experienced. His anger is a result of going against what he sees as his role, based on a cultural directive. He is *supposed* to earn more than his wife does. If you asked Peter where he got this idea, he would probably have difficulty pinpointing the source of the message. He might say he learned it from his father. He did, to be sure. His father was the primary wage earner in the family, so that is what Peter observed to be the role of a husband and father as he grew up. All the other men in his neighborhood also went out to work every day to earn money for their families. What Peter learned from listening to and watching his father and the other men reinforced a cultural message that has been accepted for generations: Men are supposed to be the primary wage earners. Such cultural directives have been operating for a long time. They affect us in subtle and not-so-subtle ways.

THE ORIGIN OF CULTURAL DIRECTIVES

Culture has been defined as an ongoing pattern of life that has been operating for generations. Where did it get its start? Our society, like just about every other society in the modern world, is based on the old patriarchal model. Under this model, males have the power. Males are supposed to be in charge; they run the nation and the family. Most importantly, they control the money. They aren't necessarily better at it, and they may not particularly like doing it; they do it because they are supposed to. Their culture tells them so.

If we take a look at culture from this historical perspective, we can see where some of our ideas about men, women, and money developed. The "male as breadwinner" and "female as homemaker" roles had their roots in the changes brought about by the Industrial Revolution starting in the 1700's. As men moved from the farm to factories to earn a living, women were left to manage the home and raise the children. Men and women's roles became separate and distinct. And men's work began to be seen as more valuable because it brought tangible rewards in the form of wages. Men were in charge, especially of the money. After all, they earned it.

When you are in charge, you have the power to make the laws. Some U.S. laws that may have made sense in the context of the times when they were written now seem pretty silly and unfair. Women have only been able to vote in the United States since 1926 and have only been able to own property in their own names in all states since 1964. In the past divorce was difficult and in many cases impossible in this country. Women had few rights because traditionally they were expected to go from their father's home to their husband's home. They always, in theory anyway, had someone to take care of them. This caretaking included someone else—a husband, father, or brother—being in control of the purse strings. Men were responsible for earning, spending, and saving the family money. This was how society was expected to run, and for the most part, it did. These were the patterns established by the culture, and they continued for generations.

Of course, there have always been women and men who didn't follow the rules society set up. Culture provides general guidelines about how things are supposed to be, but individual family messages or exceptional circumstances can override the cultural directives. So there were always men who couldn't or didn't handle money, and there were always women who knew about money, ran businesses, and became wealthy and powerful. But generally, the model of the male in charge of finances prevailed. And this is where some of our current patterns got their start.

But times have changed. We've been through the Feminist Revolution of the 1970's. Women are in the workforce and have unprecedented economic power. Men and women share responsibility and decision-making power on the job and at home. Same-sex couples are finding increasing acceptance in both the social and economic spheres. But, curiously, we still find many of our cultural directives rooted in that old concept of the male-in-charge. And these old directives play themselves out in ways that continue to shape our views of money. Couples can experience discomfort as the old ideas, often hidden in the unconscious, push against new realities in areas such as who earns more, who is in charge of the finances, and how money is saved and spent. Let's see if any of these areas affect your relationship.

THE PATRIARCHAL LEGACY—WHO EARNS MORE?

One of the major legacies of this old male-in-charge cultural pattern can be seen in our expectations about who should earn more. We still expect men to make more money than women do. A recent survey conducted by the University of Iowa found only 40 percent of the men polled believe that men and women should provide equal amounts of money to the family budget; the other 60 percent think the male should contribute more.[1] This notion has been a part of our cultural belief system for so long that we have difficulty moving away from it. "It's ingrained in their DNA to be the breadwinner," says Cheryl Broussard, a financial and small-business information consultant, discussing her work with men.[2]

In the groups we've lead, we've heard participants, both male and female, express similar discomfort with the idea of a woman earning more than a man. We have even spoken with women who tell us that they don't disclose the amount of their income because they don't want their husbands to be upset about being outearned. "He sees the amount when we file our taxes," one woman said. "But that's the only time it comes up. The rest of the time, we simply don't discuss it. The less said, the better for our relationship." We have heard this from enough couples to know this is a fairly common occurrence. Marriage and family therapists report that the issue of women outearning men is one that frequently contributes to marital discord.

The reality today is that one in three married women does make more money than her partner.[3] The days of men consistently outearning women are fading fast. We know that logically. But because individuals change more rapidly than the culture as a whole, we sometimes find ourselves caught between the old beliefs and the new realities. When our beliefs have not caught up with our behaviors, we can find ourselves uncomfortable without really understanding why. The discomfort we sometimes feel about women earning more than men is an example of being stuck in an unexamined belief from the past. And when we get stuck, we stir up a host of illogical emotions, from fear to hurt to anger, that can damage our relationship. By taking the emotion out of the issue, we can look at these expectations from a clearheaded perspective.

Do Old Expectations Affect Your Relationship?
Take a minute to look at your relationship with your partner and ask yourself:

Who earns more?

Are you both comfortable with that situation?

What did your cultural directives tell you about who was *supposed* to earn more?

If you are not following your cultural directives, how do you feel about that?

Is there anything you need to do to become more comfortable with the way things are in your relationship?

By answering these questions and sharing your conclusions with your partner, you can begin to redesign your relationship based on reality, not on an outmoded belief about the way things are supposed to be.

Does it make logical sense for a male to be expected to earn more than a female? Is functioning from some outmoded belief helpful for a relationship? The answer, clearly, is no. Any couple will be better served by recognizing these old expectations for what they are and moving beyond them.

THE PATRIARCHAL LEGACY—WHO IS IN CHARGE OF THE MONEY?

Deciding who controls the money in a relationship is another issue that often is influenced by old cultural messages. Because men have traditionally been in charge of the money in the past, some couples expect that this is the way things should continue to be. "When I marry, I want my husband to take care of the money," reported a young college student. "That's his job." When asked why she thought managing the family finances was part of his job description, she was unable to answer. "Men always manage the money" was all she could come up with. Unconsciously, she knows that generations of men have been in charge of and have managed the money for their families. Her response illustrates how strong some of the old cultural directives can be. If she observed her father and all the men in her culture taking care of the family finances, it follows that she would believe that this is the way things are supposed to be. She had absorbed this cultural message without really questioning it. More importantly, she was so locked into this directive that she didn't give herself and her partner the opportunity to decide whether or not this pattern was really appropriate for them as a couple.

Some couples are still pulled by the old cultural directives emotionally, even though both contribute financially to the family. Old directives are strong and powerful. They take conscious thought and hard work to overcome. This struggle over who is in charge of the money is one of the most common reasons that couples seek therapy, according to marriage therapists.

Sharing the Responsibility

Couples need to clarify their views on the cultural directives regarding who is in charge of the money so that they can make choices that are appropriate for their own relationship without being distracted by the old messages. If their choices go against the traditional cultural directives, they should be prepared to deal with some negative feedback from friends and relatives. Mark reported that his male friends teased him about "being henpecked" when he mentioned that his wife, Karen, handled the money in their household. "She is simply better at it than I am. She likes to do it and I find it really boring," he said. "Still, the teasing makes me uncomfortable."

Many couples are writing new money directives for themselves. In a 1998 *Working Woman* survey, over two thirds of the women responding said that they are in charge of the family finances.[4] A more egalitarian pattern is emerging for many couples, and handling money has become a shared responsibility. Couples need to constantly evaluate old directives to see if they truly fit who they are today.

Again, take a minute to look at who is in charge of the finances in your relationship. Did you discuss who would be in charge or did it just happen? Is this pattern based on what is best for you as a couple? Are you both comfortable with the way things are handled? Do your patterns fit who you are today? What do you need to do to make your relationship serve you better? By sharing the answers to these questions in a loving, supportive atmosphere, you can design a relationship that fits you as a unique couple.

THE PATRIARCHAL LEGACY—WHO SAVES, WHO SPENDS?

Saving, spending, and investing patterns can also be influenced by the old patriarchal roles and their accompanying messages. See if any of these patterns affect your relationship.

Spending

Men's and women's differing spending patterns are linked to the differing cultural messages they receive throughout their lives. Women are raised to nurture, so when they spend they are more likely to buy things for the home or their children—they tend to spend to enhance their families' daily lives. This reflects what researchers have called women's *now-money* orientation. Men's cultural directives tell them to fix and provide, so their spending is more likely to reflect accumulating value, *a future-money* orientation. Men are more likely to spend on big items, things that can be seen as an investment in the future—cars and computers, for example.[5]

Recent research found some interesting quirks in the spending habits of men and women. When something good happens to women, they tend to shop to celebrate. When something bad happens, they shop to cheer themselves up. And women buy more impulsively than men do: 36 percent of the women surveyed reported that they would buy something when they didn't need it, while only 18 percent of the men said they would. In addition, 24 percent of the women surveyed said they would buy something because it was on sale; only 5 percent of the men said they would.[6]

Men, according to researchers from Iowa State University, are more serious about their purchases. You probably won't catch them shopping to celebrate. Nor will men shop to cheer themselves up. And they seem to buy on impulse only rarely. But they do something just as intriguing. Men tend to see their wants as needs. So buying a new computer, for example, becomes a necessity rather than a desire. "I need that because it is faster than my old one, and it has more features," a man might say.[7]

These differences in spending patterns are neither right nor wrong. They are simply different responses to our cultural directives. Understanding this can help minimize conflicts that occur in relationships.

Saving

Cultural directives show up in saving patterns as well. Men are more likely to save with that future orientation in mind. They save for retirement. Women have been taught to take care of others, so they tend not to save for their own retirement, but for their children's education. Their own future comes last. Again, these patterns are based on old male-female roles. As provider, the man was trained to look toward the future, while the woman was more focused on the day-to-day concerns of the family. These old patterns are leftovers from the past, not necessarily what works best for the family today. Couples need to make plans for the future based on what works for them, not on old patterns that may no longer reflect today's reality.

Investing

Investing is another way the old sex-role patterns are played out. According to Ruth Hayden, a financial planner, "Women have been taught to invest in lifestyle and children. Men have been taught to invest in things that hold value—a house, retirement."[8] From a historical perspective, men have more experience handling money than women do because they have been doing it longer. A recent survey of unmarried Americans ages 21 to 34 found interesting differences. Forty-seven percent of the women surveyed reported that they "are not very knowledgeable about investing," while only 33 percent of the men made the same claim. Forty-four percent of the women rated their money-management skills at 5 or less on a 10-point scale, while 39 percent of the men did the same.[9] Women, unless they are involved with an investment club, tend to turn to family and friends for financial advice and are less likely to use the services of a financial planner. Generally, men tend to be more comfortable with money than women are and have more self-confidence when it comes to investing. This is another holdover from the old patriarchal culture, and while it is beginning to change, women still need to leave the old pattern behind and catch up to current realities.

Interestingly, women have been able to break the old cultural messages when they participate in investment clubs. When investment clubs are made up of all women, we see new patterns emerging. With the mutual support and encouragement women can provide each other in this format, women learn to think in new ways and find there is indeed strength in numbers. All-female investment clubs tend to outperform all-male clubs, proving that we can rewrite these old cultural messages.[10]

Patterns in Your Relationship

Take this opportunity to look at the existing saving, investing, and spending patterns in your relationship. Do you have shared goals? What do you need to do to take charge of your spending, saving, and investing patterns? How can you work more cooperatively to make your financial future what you want it to be?

The past will continue to have a hold over us as long as we automatically accept the way things have always been done. Once we give ourselves the option of making new choices based on what works for our families, we strengthen our relationships and ourselves.

At this point, we recommend that you take a minute to think about the directives your culture gave you about men's and women's roles. Be especially aware of the messages regarding money. You can use the following questions to guide your search. When you have completed your answers, share them with your partner.

What role messages came from my culture? How did my ethnic background influence these messages? How did my religious background influence these messages? How active are these messages in my life today?

What messages regarding money and couples came from my culture? How did my ethnic background influence these messages? How did my religious background influence these messages? How active are these messages in my life today?

What other observations can I make about cultural messages? What changes do I want to make?

CULTURAL DIRECTIVES IN CHILDHOOD

Even before we are born, our culture has big plans for us. And many of these plans depend on whether we are male or female. It's not unusual for expectant parents to say, "We are so excited that we are having a boy. We are such big sports fanatics, he'll fit right into this family." Or, "According to the ultrasound, we're going to have a little girl. I can't wait to shop for cute little dresses." All these expectations are established before we even make our appearance into the world! Once we arrive, they are translated into behaviors. The behaviors of adults set the stage for boys and girls to have different life experiences and to feel the effect of some powerful cultural directives.

Parents and other caregivers, responding to their cultural directives about what male and female behaviors should be like, tend to perceive little girls and little boys as being quite different, whether they truly are or not. In one interesting experiment, infants were randomly labeled with a male or female name, and then paired with an adult who had been instructed to just observe the baby. Regardless of the actual sex of the baby, the infants labeled as male were perceived as more "masculine" and stronger than those labeled as female. In another experiment, adults were asked to play with babies. The same baby was dressed as a little girl and then as a little boy. The participants in the experiment behaved differently depending on which sex child they thought they were playing with. Little boys tended to be handled more roughly; adults played with them more actively and spoke to them in louder voices. Little girls, in contrast, were cuddled more and spoken to in quiet, gentle tones. Apparently we believe we see gender differences, even in infants. We then act accordingly, attributing different characteristics to boys and girls. These perceived differences lead to different treatment based on gender. Children then respond to the way they are treated. Thus, cultural directives are passed along without conscious thought from parent to child, leading us to behave in the ways the culture tells us to do.

Based on their cultural directives, adults are frequently more protective of girls than of boys, and this is reflected in the jobs that we allow our children to take as they grow up. Think about the jobs you held as a youngster. If you are female, it is quite likely that your first paid job was as babysitter, working close to home. Males are more likely to have held more active jobs outside the home environment. Parents tend to give their adolescent boys more freedom than their adolescent girls, and this is especially true of part-time jobs. And boys generally make more money than girls do. A recent survey of wages for summer jobs conducted by Junior Achievement found that nationwide among 16- to 19-year-olds, males earned an average of $9 per hour while females earned an average of $5.25. The lessons start early! Boys learn to go out into the world and expect more money for what they do. According to most studies, they get it.

In addition to being more protective of girls than boys, we also teach them different life skills and behaviors. A number of studies on playground and classroom behaviors have found that we encourage one set of behaviors for boys and another for girls. Boys learn to speak out, girls are encouraged to be quiet. Boys engage in more active play, girls tend to be more subdued. Boys' games are more competitive and involve larger groups than those of girls. According to family therapist Betty Carter, "Boys learn about hierarchy from day one. They understand that the guy with the most power wins. Girls are taught to be nice."[11] Now we are not saying that each and every child absorbs these messages equally. Of course there are variations. But, in general, these messages about power and "being nice" are part of society's training for boys and girls. And the messages are frequently acted out in relationships, particularly when it comes to money.

Patterns From Your Childhood
How did your cultural directives shape your early behaviors? Think about the first jobs you held as a youngster.

Did your jobs fit the typical male/female pattern? Why or why not?

How did your family feel about your job?

How do you think gender affected your work beliefs? Do you see any influences on your career choice today?

THE MEDIA AND CULTURAL DIRECTIVES

The family is a powerful purveyor of cultural directives. We feel the effects of those directives every day. For all its power, however, the family frequently takes a backseat to the media in the sheer number and force of the messages passed along. We watch television, videos, and the movies. We surf the Internet. We read books, newspapers, and magazines. Words and pictures telling us what we are expected to do and be as males and females surround us. Whether we accept or reject this information, we can't ignore its pull. And the messages affect our money behaviors and beliefs.

What We See on Television

Television is a prime example of how we acquire cultural money messages. For better or worse, television has a major impact on our ideas concerning gender roles. We are exposed to countless hours of programs and commercials that help shape our beliefs about how we are supposed to behave. By the time the average person graduates from high school, he or she has viewed 15,000 hours of television. Contrast this with 11,000 hours spent in a classroom and you begin to get an idea of the hold that television has on us.[12]

Spend a couple of evenings watching prime-time TV and take note of the roles presented to us. Pay particular attention to the roles of men and women regarding work and money. Here is what you will probably see: on TV, women who work are mostly young, thin, and attractive. Working men are shown in greater variety of guises—they can be young or old, fat or thin. With a few exceptions, most of the people with power and money are male. And these powerful men are probably coupled with young women. Even in the commercials, men are depicted as being more powerful. A recent study of television commercials found that the male characters were more developed and complex than their feminine counterparts. Not only that, but men were more often shown in occupations, while women were found in the home. As we all know, commercials are meticulously designed to convince and persuade.

NBC's award-winning comedy series *Frasier* gives us an example of the male/female role images seen on television. In this popular sit-com, the male characters, Frasier Crane and his brother, Niles, are wealthy. Both have medical degrees. Their father, Martin, is a retired police officer who was wounded on duty. There are two main female characters. Roz, a single mother, is the producer of Frasier's radio talk show. We don't know much about her educational or professional background, but we do see her struggling for money. As an audience, we know more about her sex life than we do about her work life.

Daphne, the second female character on the show, is Martin's healthcare worker and Niles's current love interest. She is shown making minor attempts at cooking and cleaning around the house and occasionally is seen helping Martin with his physical therapy. Like Roz, we know more about Daphne's relationships with men than we do about other aspects of her life. Work is not a priority for either of the female characters. Nor do they have the same wealth as the men on the show. Both the women fit the standards for female beauty prevalent in society. They look great and that seems to be all that is really expected of them. These are powerful messages absorbed by everyone who watches the show.

Other television shows have similar patterns. There are some exceptions, of course, but for the most part, the patterns identified by media researchers hold true. Take a minute to list your three favorite television shows and then identify the roles they model. You may have to stand back and take a hard look at just what cultural stereotypes are being portrayed. These messages can be subtle be-cause we are so used to them. There is a high probability that your favorite TV shows also highlight unrealistic career and money roles, and that they show males and females in a different light.

What We See in Films
We mentioned *Titanic* at the beginning of this chapter. This was a major blockbuster movie of the late 1990's. Again, the pattern of powerful men and financially dependent women is continued. Rose,

the heroine, owed her life's accomplishments to Jack, her first love. Was *Titanic* an entertaining movie? Certainly. Did it continue to reinforce the female/male roles prevalent in this culture? When you consider the number of young girls who saw the movie multiple times, the answer has to be a resounding yes.

Think of the movies you have seen recently. How many include positive, powerful women's roles? How many of the female characters out-earn men? Of these successful women characters, how many were truly positive, healthy role models? Your answers to these questions will probably illustrate the subtle roles we are exposed to on a daily basis.

Your Media Directives

Television and movies are entertainment, not real life. We all know that. The roles we see portrayed on television and in movies don't absolutely determine our behavior. They do influence it, however. Why else would advertisers spend hours designing commercials to sell products? Why else would sponsors pump huge sums of money into shows they believe will have mass audience appeal? We know that the media impacts our lives. The impact is both subtle and pervasive. So any attempt to look at our roles, especially concerning money, would be incomplete without first seeing how the media affects our view of the world and ourselves.

To help you identify the cultural directives you may have received from the media, we ask you do the following:

List your two favorite television shows as a child. What do you remember about the female/male work and money roles?

List two favorite television shows today. Can you identify any stereotypical patterns in these shows? How does money fit in?

Think of the three most recent movies you have seen. What female/male roles were depicted? What behaviors were modeled regarding money behaviors?

Which of these images fits for you? Which of these images does not fit for you?

When you have finished, share your perceptions with your partner. What role has the images presented by the media played in shaping your beliefs? What changes would you like to make?

CHALLENGING CULTURAL DIRECTIVES

By now you have a good idea of how cultural messages influence your views of yourself and your relationship. You may even have identified some changes you would like to make. For Margo and Peter, the couple we profiled earlier, being able to see their cultural messages was a key to understanding their interpersonal dynamics and cutting down on the number of fights they were having. Margo was able to accept Peter's struggle over earning less than she did. She became more careful about her purchases and included Peter in the decision-making process when they involved joint funds. Peter, in turn, could see that he was really acting from his cultural messages instead of his current belief system. Once he understood the source of his discomfort, he was able to let go of much of the embarrassment he felt about not earning as much money as Margo earns. While he is still not totally comfortable with their income differences, he is able to filter out irrelevant emotions while dealing with the financial issues he and Margo must face. This gives him the opportunity to evaluate each expenditure from a logical point of view. Margo and Peter are feeling more positive about their relationship, especially since they can now stop a fight before it gets started and have a discussion instead.

Peter also had to learn to deal with the possible reactions—or perceived reactions—of his friends and family to Margo's higher income. While some might criticize or ridicule him about the situation, we would wonder what reason anyone would have for maintaining a close relationship with such people. The second possibility was that Peter might project his fears onto his friends, a common dynamic. If he didn't want to deal with his judgments about his own behavior, he could decide that his friends were judging him. This would keep him trapped in his culturally prescribed behaviors and beliefs. But fortunately for both Peter and Margo, he was willing to resolve his internal conflict to the point where he was not concerned about friends' and family members' reactions.

When we can identify the messages and accompanying role expectations we receive from our culture, we give ourselves more and healthier options. We can chose new roles or follow the old ones, based on what works best for our relationship. We function from choice rather than old, programmed behaviors. This process of conscious choice gives us new power and strengthens our relationships. By understanding the subtle pull of old messages, we have the opportunity, like Margo and Peter, to design a way of functioning that fits us as a couple. We can stop having fights and have discussions instead. In doing so, we increase cooperation, focus on our joint goals, and take our relationship to a new level. We invite you to do the same as you look at the cultural messages you carry with you.

MOVING FORWARD

When we ask you to look at your cultural messages, we are encouraging you to make some conscious choices about what is true for you and your partner. Messages that you have grown up with may not fit the person you are today. And they may not work for the relationship you want to build with your partner. Redesigning these directives gives you the power to decide what works for you, rather than just blindly accepting past beliefs and habits.

Here are some steps to take in assessing old messages and developing new ones. You can work individually at first, and then share your insights with your partner when you feel you are ready.

1. List some of the cultural directives you believe have been active in your life. Decide which of these directives are still helpful and which no longer fit.

2. Identify any areas of emotional discomfort that stem from going against your cultural directives. Develop a strategy for coping with the discomfort.

3. Remind yourself that you can rewrite aspects of your culture without negating the values you think are important.

4. Carefully study your patterns of saving, spending, and investing. Now compare your patterns with those of your partner. Are

you satisfied with how things work? What changes would you like to make? How will you go about making these changes?

5. Decide which of your cultural messages are likely to complement those held by your partner. Which are likely to cause dissention? Can you see areas of possible compromise?

6. Write your thoughts in your journal, so that you can go back to them as you continue to work with your cultural directives.

PART 2

Messages in the Present

5

MONEY AND SELF-WORTH

Money and self-worth are closely intertwined. We feel on top of the world when we have it and down in the dumps when we don't. Oh, there are exceptions, of course. Mother Theresa lived her life in poverty. Her feelings of self-worth seem to have come from giving her life to the poorest of the poor in India. Other people live similar lives of self-denial and apparently thrive. Most of the rest of us, however, find the connection between money and self-worth to be a strong one. And it plays out in many areas of our lives. This money/self-worth link affects how we view others, how worthy we feel, and even whom we select as a partner. The effect money has on our self-worth may be subtle or blatant, but we have all felt its power. We are going to look at how self-worth and money came to be joined, and the various ways money connects to our feelings of self-worth as individuals and in relationships.

LEARNING THE CONNECTION

The money/self-worth connection is learned, the process beginning in childhood. Here's how it works: One of the skills we develop early in life is the ability to make comparisons. We compare ourselves to others around us and judge ourselves and them accordingly. We may be taller, smarter, or stronger than our peers, and we care about that difference because it helps us define who we are. We make similar comparisons in regard to our family and other families. These comparisons extend to money as well. We learn early on that there are variations in the amount of money that people have and that these variations are significant because they expand or limit our options. Perhaps we are told the family can't afford to go certain places or to buy the "in" fashions all the other kids have. Or we may observe that playmates have more or less than we do. These comparisons teach us where our family ranks when measured against others on an economic scale. Depending on the judgments that go along with this ranking, we feel pride or shame. Jay tells of feeling ashamed in fifth grade when he was unable to match his classmates' contributions to the charity the class had adopted. "The teacher wrote the names of students on the chalkboard as they brought in their donations from home. My family just didn't have any extra money to give to me, so I was embarrassed because my name wasn't up there. All the other kids knew that my family was too poor to contribute. I hated that."

WEALTH AND STATUS

As we go through these kinds of experiences, we begin to understand the difference money makes in our lives. Like it or not, how much money our family has determines many of our opportunities in life. The schools we attend, the social and cultural experiences open to us, even the company we keep is likely to be affected by our economic status. We also begin to understand that having money confers a higher social status than being poor. Again, we make judgments about ourselves based on these comparisons, and so money becomes linked to our feelings of self-worth.

Our society also helps to forge the link between self-worth and money. The media tells us about people who live in a grand manner, and we see their lives as somehow more interesting and important than ours. We are fascinated by "lifestyles of the rich and famous." We visit Elvis Presley's Graceland mansion and are awed by tales of his excesses. We want to know as much as we can about the activities of the late Princess Diana. Everything about her, from her romances to her wardrobe, is of interest. The Kennedy family similarly intrigues us, and we eagerly follow news of their births, deaths, and special events. We watch other wealthy celebrities jet here and there to places most of us can only dream of visiting. Our celebrity-watching culture tells us that wealth brings privilege and importance. We enjoy hearing about lives that so differ from ours and speculate what we would do if we won the lottery.

WORKING TO BE WEALTHY

Our society also values the hard work that leads to wealth, and embracing this value influences our feelings of worthiness. To call someone "self-made" is considered a high compliment. We like to read success stories, and rags-to-riches tales are always popular. We love to hear about an unknown computer nerd who started out working on some program in a basement and now is worth millions, or the cleaning lady able to save enough money to leave a substantial bequest to the college whose floors she once scrubbed. A strong thread of our American culture is the belief that, with enough effort, anyone can become rich. We value hard work and salute those who achieve wealth in this way. We view them as worthy and want to be like them. Many entrepreneurs are at least partly motivated by this belief.

On the other hand, we have little respect for people who do not work their way to financial security. Our society tends to blame people for being poor and frequently assumes that most people on welfare are "cheaters" out to milk the system. Cities with large populations of homeless people consider arresting them to get them off the streets. Some cities require those who utilize public shelters to perform some type of work in exchange for the sleeping space they are given. We developed special programs to oblige people on public assistance get into the workforce. While these actions and programs may come from good intentions, the motivating beliefs behind them are often punitive.

Being poor brings a harsh judgment upon the person: The poor person didn't work hard enough to change fate. Or was too lazy to try. Or there is just "something wrong" with them. Rightly or wrongly, poverty brings shame and negative judgements.

No wonder money and self-worth become linked in our minds. Being able to take care of ourselves financially brings independence, pride, and social approval. Being needy or dependent on others is uncomfortable and even shameful. Clearly, most of us feel good when we are contributing members of society. The work that we do earns us money and, more importantly, self-respect. Money enables us to take care of our family and ourselves, and thus it contributes to our feelings of self-worth.

MONEY/SELF-WORTH AND COUPLE DYNAMICS

This money/self-worth connection is also played out in a variety of ways in couple dynamics. We can gain a sense of self-worth by our choice of a mate. A potential partner who has money is seen as a "good catch" and thus enhances our standing. A financially struggling marriage prospect is seen as less worthy, so our standing is diminished accordingly. Pairing up with someone who is unemployed is likely to bring disapproval from family and friends. Parents naturally want their offspring to choose a relationship partner who is stable and financially secure. We want that for ourselves as well. In a recent survey, women ranked a potential mate's earning power as eighth on a list of desirable qualities. Men gave earning power a slightly lower place on their list of priorities in choosing a mate, ranking it eleventh.[1]

In general, women prefer partners who are slightly older, industrious, higher in status, and economically successful. Women, it seems, still are drawn to the good provider. Men, on the other hand, prefer partners who are younger and more physically attractive.[2]

For men, being that good provider brings approval and thus contributes to their self-worth. There are strong social expectations that men *should* take care of their families. Not living up to these expectations leads to disapproval and shame. The term "deadbeat dad" shows our highly negative judgment of men who default on their child-support obligations. To be a real man means holding down a job and providing for the family. In a recent study, 85 percent of men surveyed said that knowing they were providing well for their families offset having a job they disliked. These men could feel good about themselves even though their work life was unsatisfactory.[3]

The same standards can apply when choosing a business partner. We want to work with someone whom we see as already successful. Sometimes an individual with a weak sense of self-worth tries to go into business with a person she or he perceives as having a strong, successful relationship with money. After the success of our first books, for example, we both were approached by individuals who wanted to write a book with us or to go into private practice with us. Trying to enhance self-esteem by riding on someone else's business success is a disaster for both people. Just like any other couple, business partners are more likely to build the business they want when they both understand the relationship between money and self-worth.

Money influences mate selection in yet another way. Psychologists who study dating and mating patterns tell us that a major factor attracting people to each other is similarity. In spite of the popular belief that opposites attract, studies indicate that most couples are together because of their similarities rather than their differences. Sharing interests, religion, ethnicity, and family background all are important in our selection of potential partners. This being the case, we are likely to link up with mates of similar economic status. And choosing partners who are more like us gives our relationship a better chance of survival.

When a person doesn't select a partner from a similar economic background, it is enough of a deviation to be remarkable. The romance between people of vastly different incomes forms the major story line of numerous movies. In *Titanic,* a rich girl and a poor boy fall in love and encounter family displeasure because of status differences. In *Notting Hill,* a poor but charming bookseller and a wealthy film star struggle with the discrepancies in lifestyle and economics. Two wealthy brothers vie for the affections of the chauffeur's daughter in *Sabrina.* The prostitute and the wealthy executive find love in *Pretty Woman.* These differences in economic status make for interesting fantasy stories. Love conquers all in romantic movies. The reality is quite different. Marriage and family counselors often see such couples for therapy and are well aware that differences in financial background can bring problems as people from two different backgrounds attempt to blend their lives.

When committed relationships break up, money and self-worth are connected in ways that can seem strange. In the case of a bitter divorce, money frequently becomes a way to heal bruised self-esteem. So while many divorce battles may look like fights over money, they are really attempts to strengthen a battered sense of worth. In the novel and later movie *First Wives Club,* four jilted wives concoct a plot to bilk their errant husbands of their money to obtain revenge. The women's self-esteem and confidence increases as a result of their financial triumph. We remember seeing a license plate on the back of an expensive sports car that let everyone know who won in this divorcing couple's money dispute—the plate read "WasHis."

When older men divorce, assuming they are sufficiently wealthy, they may acquire what has come to be known as a "trophy wife." Supposedly the man's view of himself is enhanced when he marries woman much younger than the wife he left. The younger woman usually is attracted to his power and money. We seldom hear of "trophy husbands." Given our cultural history of women marrying good providers, it is okay for women to hook up with powerful wealthy older men. This type of union could certainly raise the self-esteem of both people. But when the reverse happens we are taken aback. The "younger" man will most likely face ridicule and social sanctions. In all likelihood, this couple will not enjoy the slap-on-the-back, wink-of-an-eye approval from family and friends that would be granted the older man–younger woman combination.

GENDER DIFFERENCES REGARDING MONEY AND SELF-WORTH

Some gender differences exist in the link between money and self-worth. Many of these are tied into our cultural messages, so you may wish to review Chapter 4. In general, men's sense of self-worth is more closely tied to the work they do than is women's. It has been said that masculinity is measured by the size of a paycheck. Beginning at an early age, men are socialized to measure their identity by the work they do. Work and self-worth become tightly entwined. This is especially apparent when there is a sudden loss of income.

"Losing my job was the lowest point in my life. When the mines closed and I was thrown out of work, I was surprised at how hard it was to handle my feelings. I had gone from making good money to sitting home reading the want ads. When I had to check in at the unemployment office I felt like I was wearing a big sign that said 'loser.' I was depressed, angry and most of all, ashamed. I felt like I had lost my value as a person." As he described his four-month period of unemployment, Cal kept his eyes downcast and spoke softly. Clearly, even though he had found other work as a security guard, the shame of being unemployed still rankled.

Nora, his wife, shared her perspective. "That was such a difficult time for us. I tried to be supportive and encouraging. But he just withdrew into himself. He was crabby and short-tempered with me and the children. I don't think he meant to take it out on us, but it felt like that's what he was doing. It took us awhile to get back on track even after he had a job again."

Nora and Cal aren't alone. When a partner loses a job, it usually throws a couple into a crisis. A prolonged period of unemployment just adds to the misery. Many couples, whether heterosexual or homosexual, report that such periods were the most difficult, stressful times in their relationship. Some programs that provide retraining for laid-off workers acknowledge this difficulty by offering family counseling as well as job-seeking assistance. Unfortunately, when same-sex couples are not viewed as a family, they may not be eligible for this important benefit.

Unemployment *is* a crisis for couples, but lack of money is just part of the problem. What is usually at the heart of the conflict is a feeling of low self-worth. If a person believes that his or her self-worth is defined by a paycheck, it stands to reason that when that paycheck is lost, so is the person's sense of self-worth. Psychiatrist Gerald Rozansky says: "When you lose your wealth, for some, it becomes the loss of one's self-esteem."[4] The self-worth/money connection seems to be especially strong for men. A recent study speaks to this connection. Research done at a major university found that having money makes a man feel loveable, happy, and in control. Further, men appear to envy those who earn a great deal of money, and rate people with money as more attractive, responsible, and rational than those without money.[5]

While we acknowledge that the money/self-worth connection is also present in many career-oriented women, the women in this same study showed an interesting difference in attitudes from the men. Instead of rating people with money positively as the men did, they reported feeling repelled and intimidated by those who earn a lot of money. Women also revealed that earning more money than their parents would make them feel guilty. "Money and the self are interwoven for men and women, but the weavings result in a different pattern," conclude the researchers.[6]

The challenge presented by this differing pattern is that each partner must come to understand the other's beliefs as they apply to money and self-worth. For example, suppose one partner derives her self-esteem from living according to her values, while the other partner's sense of self is tied to working and earning money. If the first person loses her job, she may need support and encouragement as she seeks to find another job that matches her values. Her partner, however, may think he is being supportive by urging her to get another job as quickly as possible—after all, that's what he would do to reinforce his self-esteem in a similar situation. Unless these two have a thorough discussion about her beliefs concerning money and self-worth, she will think he's being unsupportive, while he will become frustrated and may begin to question whether she really wants another job! This dynamic can happen in both straight and gay couples.

These different patterns were reflected in a study of debt and bankruptcy conducted by a researcher at Iowa State University. Professor Tahira K. Hira found some interesting gender differences in the kinds of debt people accumulated. The men studied often got into debt by buying things for themselves and were still paying for cars they no longer owned when they filed for bankruptcy. The women in the study tended to get into debt by hooking up with men who needed financial help. "We noticed in the women's cases, many were becoming attached to men who needed picking up and cleaning up. Then the man would walk away and they would pick up another puppy who was bruised." What men and women had in common in this study was that those with unmanageable debt also displayed low self-esteem. "In both cases, these people were trying to prove something to themselves," Professor Hira said. Those in debt reported unstable family backgrounds and difficult family and school relationships.[7] This is not surprising—an unstable family background affects our sense of self-worth, and self-worth affects our dealings with money.

Family background, self-worth, and money appear to be connected in another way. Some recent research has uncovered the fact that a disproportional number of women on welfare were sexually abused as children. Although figures on sexual abuse are difficult to pin down, most experts agree that from 20 to 25 percent of women in the general population have been sexually abused.[8] Among women on welfare, the median figure from a number of studies reveals a higher rate of sexual abuse—33 percent. The women in this study were found to have difficulty dealing with authority and displayed an underlying pattern of "conflict, defiance and flight."[9] This pattern affects a person's ability to get and keep a job, as well as to stay out of debt. We know that adults abused as children have many issues to deal with in their healing process. Self-worth and money issues appear to be another piece of the puzzle.

OCCUPATION, MONEY, AND SELF-WORTH

How we earn money is yet another factor in the money/self-worth connection. We have seen that we judge others and ourselves by how much money they and we make. We also judge and are judged by how that money is made.

Imagine yourself at a party. You don't know anyone except your host, so you are trying to connect and feel comfortable. As you move through the crowd, you make contact by smiling, nodding, and trying to appear as pleasant as possible. You spot a person you think looks interesting and you strike up a conversation. You probably start by discussing the weather or how you know the host. After a few surface pleasantries, one of you will probably continue your conversation with some variation of the question "So, what do you do?" How often have you asked or been asked this question? Probably more times than you can count. Why is it one of the first questions we ask when we meet someone? Why is it so important to us to know someone's occupation? In many other cultures, getting to know someone initially revolves around finding out what family connections that person has. The individual is at least partly understood within her or his family context. The culture of the United States, however, places great emphasis on how the person earns a living.

When we ask "What do you do?" we are gathering basic information about the person we have just met. Once we learn what a person does, we may see some commonalities and shared interests. Or we can decide that we probably do not want to pursue this acquaintance any further. Work is such an important part of who we are in this culture that most of us seek to know others through knowing the work they do. Knowing someone's work provides us with a quick method of classifying and judging others in relation to ourselves.

We all have preconceived notions about people based on their work. Your response to hearing that someone you just met sells used cars, is a college professor, or works with AIDS patients may be positive or negative, depending on your past experience and your own way of making a living. But your response will not be neutral. As soon as we hear someone's occupation, we make some judgment. We form impressions of people as more or less worthy, depending on how we perceive the work they do.

If we judge others by the work they do and the money they make, it follows that we also judge ourselves according to these same factors. For most of us, work and self-worth are closely linked. And this connection plays out in our relationship as a couple. So what happens when our relationships in this area are less than equal? Do we experience problems when one partner outearns the other? Or has a more prestigious job? Or decides to stay home to raise the children? Does the lower-earning partner feel less worthy? In some relationships, this inequality can cause problems. One expert believes that this issue is even more difficult for gay couples than for straight couples. "For same-sex partners, income disparities may be linked to such factors as class, ability, attitude, ambition, and personality, all of which are very explosive topics."[10]

Couples can work these discrepancies out with love and open communication.

SPENDING AND SELF-WORTH

Money and self-worth are linked in another important way—how and what we spend our money on. We frequently buy items to enhance our feelings of self-worth. Advertisers count on this fact when they pay out huge sums to let us know that certain items will enhance our worthiness. "It costs more but I'm worth it," ads for a certain hair product tell us.

We all recognize other brand names that come with prestige already attached: Brooks Brothers, Armani, Cartier, Rolex, Mercedes-Benz, Cadillac. All these brands are advertised in such a way as to let us know that we are worthier if we buy them. We are also told that people will like us better if we drink certain beers or eat at certain restaurants. Advertising is a constant in our lives, making it difficult to sort out truth from fiction.

So we think we can enhance our self-worth by what we buy. We have already talked about the fact men and women spend differently. And that men and women with debt problems get to that point for different reasons. Researcher Tahira Hira says, "We spend because others are doing it. Women have more need to be accepted by others. Maybe they think that if they have the things that others have, they'll be better off, they'll be liked and accepted."[11] A survey commissioned by Oppenheimer Funds Inc. supports this idea of spending to be accepted. Researchers found that 75 percent of single women polled said that it is important to look successful. In keeping with this desire to look a certain way, 54 percent of young women polled were more likely to acquire 30 pairs of shoes before saving $30,000 in retirement assets. Researchers have called this the "Carrie Bradshaw Syndrome" after the character on the television show *Sex and the City* whose focus is on looking good and spending, not saving.[12]

Men also spend to impress others, they just do it differently. As we have mentioned before, men are more likely to spend on big-ticket items like cars and electronic equipment. Regarding men's spending, financial counselor Ruth Hayden says, "They spend really big to show off because there's a lot of ego risk on men today to do better than the next guy."[13]

Both women and men may find themselves trying to bolster their self-worth as parents by spending money on their offspring. This can be a major problem for any couple, but it's especially trouble-some when the children are from a previous marriage. We are all familiar with situations in which the noncustodial parent gives the children lavish gifts and spends lots of money on entertainment during visits. Even after the children leave home, the problems have a way of resurfacing. Rhoda told this story:

"This is a second marriage for both of us. I don't have any children, so it is really difficult for me to identify with Kirk's need to provide for his 23-year-old daughter, who is still in college. She is always coming to him so he can bail her out of her financial holes. Because he feels guilty about his divorce and not being there for her when she was growing up, he gives her whatever she asks for. I worked my way through college, and I just can't see why he won't make her do the same. He says it makes him feel good to be able to help her out. I say he needs to kick her out of the nest and concentrate on our relationship. He spends way too much on her needs and then finds himself financially strapped."

Whether you are male or female, spending patterns that are an attempt to bolster self-worth can be problematic. Individuals who spend for all the wrong reasons can find themselves chasing in an endless circle. In addition, this kind of spending can take a major toll on a relationship. Partners end up resentful, angry, and disconnected from each other, so their self-worth takes another hit. They then might be tempted to spend more to relieve the bad feelings from the fights and distancing. What a vicious cycle!

This same dynamic holds true for business partners who may feel the need to spend profits lavishly on themselves to enhance their self-esteem. Profits that ought to be going back into building the business are instead siphoned off to fulfill an unmet emotional need. Such business partners need to have frank discussions and clear agreements regarding spending company profits.

CHANGING YOUR PATTERNS

How can couples find ways to end these destructive patterns? Here are some steps we recommend:

1) **Raise your awareness.** Take a minute to think about the last time you spent money on a nonessential purchase. By nonessential, we mean items other than your basic living expenses such as food, housing, and utilities. What did you buy? Why did you buy it? Was there a need you were trying to fill with this purchase? What was it? Now share this information with your partner and compare notes. Do you see any patterns in your spending? Are there any ways you are trying to bolster your feelings of self-worth?

2) **Change your patterns.** For the next month, practice the tactic of conscious spending. Use only cash, not credit cards, for your purchases. This will make you more conscious of exactly how much you really are spending. Every time you purchase something, take a minute to ask yourself "What need am I trying to fill here?" Then if you decide you really want the item, buy it consciously. Take a minute to calculate how many hours you work to pay for this item. Is it worth it? If you decide it is, pay with cash, counting your money out slowly for the clerk.

By taking the conscious-spending approach, you will get more information about yourself and your reasons for spending. This will allow you to make choices based on reality instead of emotions. You may still choose to buy, but now you will know why. You will feel better about yourself, and your relationship will be healthier as a result.

Michele told us how using this method worked for her:

"My intent was to buy a blouse to go with my gray suit. I had several items in the dressing room with me and so as I tried them on, I asked myself what need I was trying to fill. My insecurity about the presentation I was scheduled to make on Wednesday hit me with a major jolt. I realized that along with a blouse, I was also trying to buy some self-confidence, because I was really intimidated by the group I'd be speaking to. The Conscious Spending Exercise surprised me, because I didn't really see what was going on for me and how insecure I felt. I realized that I didn't need a new blouse. I needed to go over my figures for my presentation to be as prepared as I could possibly be. The fringe benefit of this realization was that I didn't have to explain to my partner why I exceeded our budget yet again. When I told her about my experience, I got a big congratulatory hug. That felt good, too."

DEVELOPING A HEALTHY DEFINITION OF SELF-WORTH

Once we begin to understand how money and self-worth are connected, we can begin to redefine ourselves in more healthy ways. At this point you might wish to look back at your genograms and the information you gained from the chapter on cultural messages. What money/self-worth connections do you see as part of your past? How many of those messages are still active today? Which do you want to change? Which ones do you wish to keep?

One good way to make sure your definition of self-worth incorporates those messages you want it to is to look ahead to the future. Ask yourself, "How do I want to be remembered when I leave this earth?" If you were writing your own obituary, how would you want to see the following sentences completed?

At the time of his death, he was working on becoming _____.
The world will suffer the loss of her contributions in the areas of _____.

He will be mourned by _____ because _____.

She recently fulfilled a lifelong dream of _____.

Her partner will miss her greatly because _____.

Your answers to these questions will probably not include how much money you made and spent in your lifetime.

Make no mistake. Money *is* important. It allows us to fulfill our life purpose and to have security and freedom from worrying about how to pay the rent and put food on the table. But money doesn't define our worth as an individual. It cannot make us a loving partner, a supportive parent, a better businessperson, or a contributing community member. Putting money in its proper perspective allows us to focus on what is really important and to have a more realistic definition of self-worth. Money is a tool—nothing more, nothing less. We encourage you to continue to develop a self-definition that does not include money. You will find that the effort pays rich dividends in your increased peace of mind and self-esteem.

MOVING FORWARD ▶▶▶▶▶▶▶▶▶

This chapter looked at the money and self-worth connection. We have seen how self-worth can develop in unhealthy ways when money becomes a part of the equation. The good news is that money and self-worth do not have to be intertwined. Developing a definition of self-worth that does not depend on money is a step toward a healthier belief system. Here are some steps for you to follow in order to establish a definition of self-worth that is not dependent on money:

1. List the messages you carry about money and self-worth. Which ones are you ready to discard? Which ones do you wish to keep?

2. List the last three times you used money to bolster your self-worth. Can you think of things you could have done instead?

3. Answer these questions: How do I want to be remembered when I die? What is the most important contribution I have made to the world in my lifetime?

4. Share your thoughts on the money/self-worth connection with your partner.

6

MONEY AND EMOTIONS

Very little in our lives stirs our emotions quite the way talking about money does, especially when our fears concerning money are provoked. The reality that money is simply a medium of exchange becomes obscured when our emotions are aroused. In minutes, we can go from being in a loving relationship to being in the midst of a loud argument complete with hurtful words fired back and forth. Our fears are activated; communication is broken down. Money has taken on a role that is way out of proportion to its actual place in our lives. Many of the exercises in this book are designed to help you detach yourself from the emotions you have about money so you and your partner can focus on the issue that needs to be resolved. We need to detach from the emotion in a way that allows us to honor our feelings, learn from them, and move on to resolving the issue that is keeping us from having the kind of relationship with money that we want, both individually and as a couple.

We realize that in writing this money guide for couples we're making an assumption: that you both want to emphasize the love in your relationship. When dealing with money, it's easy to move away from love and into a host of other, non-loving emotions. Identifying specific money issues is important, but understanding our emotional reactions to money forms the basis of a healthy relationship with it.

UNDERSTANDING EMOTIONS

While there are several different frameworks for understanding human emotions, we will use one that is gaining wide acceptance. Specifically, humans are born with an instinct to survive that gives rise to two fundamental emotions: love and fear, both at the root of virtually all other feelings. Love enables us to bond with other living beings, forming relationships that help us survive. Fear, on the other hand, warns us of danger so we can take appropriate action for self-preservation. If we delve into our feelings, we find that most of the time our emotional reactions are either love-based or fear-based. So understanding our emotions involving money means being able to separate love-based from fear-based reactions. In a partnership, it also involves a willingness to let our partner in on our emotions while understanding that person's emotional reactions to money.

The connection between love and its offspring emotions is easy to understand. We can readily see the link between love and joy or happiness or peace. But the connection between fear and the emotions that arise from it can be tougher to accept. Feelings such as anger, frustration, and anxiety, all often associated with money, can be dealt with more effectively when we make the connection to the underlying fear. Think of what you know about wild animal behavior. There's nothing more ferocious or unpredictable than an animal that believes its survival is threatened and is acting out of fear. We weren't born with any feelings about money one way or the other—we learned all of them. Yet we can react to situations that set off our money fears as if our lives were threatened. This is an important point to remember. Most of us have learned that money and fears concerning our survival go together.

One popular notion is that many couples break up because they have problems with money. A more accurate assessment is that they have unresolved money issues and their fear-based messages keep them entrenched in negative ways of relating to money. This is true regardless of whether the couple is in an intimate or a business relationship. The problem isn't with money per se, it's with individual messages and whether each person chooses to relate to money through fear or through love. Building a positive relationship with money based on love puts us in charge, rather than our fears.

We sometimes get so caught up in feeling our fears that we forget they serve a useful function. Fears are warnings—signals to pay attention to a threat. In the case of money fears, this is also true. They can give us a clear sign that we need to look at what's going on with our relationship with money. Fears can be signals that we need to look into exactly what message is being triggered and begin the process of clearing out those fears so that our relationship with money, and hence our relationship with our partner, ultimately becomes clearer and stronger. So our fears can give us a pathway for clearing out unhealthy beliefs we have learned about money. Used in this way, fears can be very helpful.

FEAR-BASED MONEY BELIEFS

There are several important points to remember about fear-based money beliefs. First, they are usually someone else's truth. They arise from that person's experience, and he or she passes them along to anyone who will listen. Children do listen to the adults around them, picking up a host of verbal and nonverbal messages. Your genogram will help you identify the fears that have been passed along in your family. For example, if your parents lived through some financial setback, you may have a fear of losing financial security. This fear may have no basis in reality for you, but because it was your parents' truth, you have absorbed it as yours. So no matter how much money you earn or the extent of your financial reserves, you will still fear a financial collapse. We had one workshop participant who kept in excess of $15,000 in her checking account, "just in case," even though she knew having that much money in a non-interest-bearing account was a poor decision financially. This behavior frustrated her partner. Once the fear behind the behavior was identified, she could, with her partner's support, learn new ways of managing the fear that were financially less costly.

Second, the more we believe something to be true, the more we behave as if it were true. We even get ourselves into situations that reinforce our beliefs, regardless of how negative they may be. We unconsciously seek out workplaces that reinforce our beliefs, and relationships that do the same. A person coming from a belief system that says resources are limited will probably end up working in an environment that is always short of resources. At the same time this person may choose a partner with the opposite belief—that money is plentiful. This individual gives him the opportunity to know what the opposing view is without having to experience it within himself. In other words, opposites attract. The behaviors arising from these differing beliefs are likely to be in conflict with each other. This couple can grow only by understanding this dynamic and making the commitment to create a healthy belief system they both share.

Third, fears are usually based on a prediction. If we can uncover the prediction, we have a better chance of understanding the fear. Suppose I am afraid of not having enough money. This fear carries the prediction that I am unable to generate adequate money to meet my bills. To make this belief true for me—we instinctively want to be right about our beliefs—I may consistently take low-paying jobs, or I might spend money beyond my income, regardless of how high it is. My prediction comes true in either case. When I understand the prediction underlying my behavior, I can begin to develop a more positive way of relating to money.

Fourth, fear-based beliefs are depowering in nature. So every time we respond from fear to a money issue, we are giving our power away. While we will talk more about money and power in Chapter 9, remember that if we are willing to give our power away, inevitably someone else will be happy to take it. Developing responses to money that are connected to love is the antidote.

Finally, many people don't like looking at the connection between fear and other emotions because it requires a willingness to be totally honest with themselves and to dig deeply for those connections. This process can be upsetting, so people sometimes conclude that it's easier to stay with their anger or their anxiety than it is to examine and heal the underlying cause. But that choice is really the more difficult one since it means stress about money will continue, as will potentially destructive behaviors. We know that one of the amazing things about being human is that we can change our behaviors, developing the kind of relationship with money and with each other that we want. So if we can look at fear as a message instead of a destructive force, we can then ask ourselves "Just what is my fear telling me? What do I need to do?"

RELATING THROUGH LOVE

Being able to identify our underlying fears involving money and to understand how those fears manifest in other emotions is critical to building a healthy partnership. Once we identify and face our fears, then we are able to move back into the energy that is love. We cannot be fearful and loving at the same time; the two energies are mutually exclusive. Our basic assumption is operating here—that you and your partner would prefer to relate to and connect with each other through love rather than fear. Certainly many relationships are founded on fear. Sometimes when we become involved in a partner-ship with another individual, we do so from an unconscious desire to have that person take our fears away. They may be able to do that in one area, but as a foundation for a meaningful relationship, this situation is disastrous, regardless of whether the relationship is an intimate primary one or a business one.

Relating to someone else through our fears gives rise to power struggles, anger, frustration, dishonesty, insecurity, defensiveness—everything we can muster to "protect" ourselves from the "threat" that is setting off our fears. With love as the foundation for a relationship, however, we are aligned with an energy force that is strong and compassionate, infinite and expansive. The feelings that arise from love are ones of joy, confidence, and an openness to embrace the love offered by our partner. Our sense of self-power is intact when we are feeling love energy, so we don't feel the need to exercise power over someone else, becoming engaged in a fruitless struggle that inevitably damages the relationship. In other words, when build-ing a healthy relationship between you and your partner and between that partnership and money, staying in love and love-charged energy gives you a high probability of success. Staying in fear and fear-charged energy dooms you.

IDENTIFYING FEARS

So how do we begin to identify the fears underlying so many of our emotional responses to money? The first step is accepting that much of the time, regardless of the immediate emotion we're feeling, our reaction to events is based on fear. Assume that your anger or frustration or anxiety about money is fear-based as you begin your attempt to understand your emotional reactions to money. If, after an honest and thorough exploration, you find that it's not, then you can just deal with that emotion. The vast majority of the time, however, a fear connection will be there. The process of dealing with emotions is essentially the same, regardless of what the specific feeling is. It's just much more effective when you are focused on the core emotion.

Let's look at some possible fear connections that might be at the root of some common emotional reactions people have to their money issues. You may find that these suggestions are right on target for you, or you may realize that different fears underlie some of your money-related emotions. If this is the case, write down your specific fears. Here are some of the emotional reactions and their underlying fears identified by workshop participants:

Greed—the fear of not getting my share; fear of poverty.

Frustration—the fear of losing control over others and/or over one's money.

Anxiety—the fear of not having enough, fear of lack; fear of not being perfect, of not "doing it right."

Anger—the fear of losing it all.

You may find that you have other emotional reactions that can be triggered by money. If so, what fears are actually set off? What predictions are connected to these fears? Keep a list of these feelings in your journal or in this book. Sometimes the fear basis will be obvious to you, and you won't have to do much more than ask yourself "What fear is underlying this emotion?" to have your answer. At other times, the connections may be more obscure; you will have to dig a bit. Going to your genogram to look at family fear patterns related to money may help you to see if you are hooked into any familial issues. Asking your partner for assistance may also be beneficial. It's often easier to see what's behind someone else's emotions than it is to interpret our own. A word of caution here: You must avoid any judgments when trying to help someone understand their emotional reactions. Also, don't be tempted to tell someone else you know for certain what she or he is feeling. Remember, your "certainty" is only a guess! Even if you are right, presenting the information in an unsupportive way will quickly shut down communication. Simply suggest that, based on how you know this individual, she or he might be plugging into this or that fear. You and your partner can best serve each other by offering support during this process. Keep the lines of communication flowing by being open, receptive, and nonjudgmental.

Letting your partner know what you discover about yourself and your emotional reactions to money is a very important step in enabling the two of you to build a relationship of trust involving money. Once you have acknowledged and faced your fears, you can move back to a place of love to resolve money conflicts. Love energy gives both of you an entirely new perspective on resolving problems. But fears have to be dealt with rather than masked behind other emotions or dismissed and buried in the fog of denial.

RESOLVING THE FEAR

Once you recognize the fear that has been evoked by a money issue, how do you resolve it? When dealing with any unhealthy emotional reaction, we recommend the following steps:

1. Understand exactly what the emotion is.

2. Know what role it plays in your life and how it has served you.

3. Discover from whom, if anyone, you learned this particular emotion.

4. Give the emotion back to that individual.

5. Replace it with an emotional response that is more appropriate.

What's the Motivation?

Step one involves the kind of searching we have been discussing—looking for the fear or love basis for the emotion so you can deal with the motivating energy behind your reaction. For example, if I get angry because my partner has overspent our budget after agreeing not to, I might understand that my anger is coming from a fear of not having enough. So I need to look at that fear in light of our reality. But I also need to deal with my anger, since it is a legitimate response to my partner's failure to honor an agreement. We need to resolve the broken-promise issue together, starting with discovering what motivated my partner to overspend. Next, I need to look at my fear of poverty. By facing the underlying fear, I can more easily deal with my anger, especially if I can move myself from fear to love. Coping with the situation that triggered my anger while staying aligned with my love energy gives me many options for resolving the issue in positive ways. I will find it much easier to listen to my partner, staying detached from my anger while honoring the validity of my reaction. We have a greater likelihood of coming to a positive resolution to the problem when we both approach the issue from a place of love than we do if one or the other of us is feeling fearful.

How Has the Fear Served You?
We've mentioned the importance of honoring your emotions; that's what step two is all about. Once you have identified an emotional reaction to a money issue, ask yourself how this response has served you. Sometimes anger is a mechanism for keeping other people away—not many people want to face an angry person. By keeping distance when it comes to money issues, an individual can avoid talking about the issue with his or her partner. Anger can also enable a person to maintain the illusion of control over money in an attempt to quiet a fear of not being in control. So the question "How does this fear (or anger or frustration) serve me?" can have more than one answer. Knowing the answer is vital, because our emotional reactions serve some need in us. The need will probably still exist, or at least it will have to be dealt with in a positive way. Once you have reached this point in your inner explorations, you are ready to ask yourself: "What else can meet this need? Do I have to have this need met?" A loving partner's input can be invaluable here.

Whose Voice Is It?
The third step, finding out who gave you the message, is important to sorting out what emotions linked to your money messages are valid for you and your experience, and which ones were learned from others. This distinction is especially critical when sorting out fear responses. Remember, we learn our fears involving money. No one is born with them. But we are born with an instinct to survive. So as you sort through your fear-based reactions to money, ask

yourself, "Whose voice do I hear saying or living out this fear? What are the exact words that person might have said to me? What behaviors did this person exhibit that reinforced this fear? Does this fear have any validity in my life?" Sometimes hanging onto old family messages is a way of maintaining loyalty to the family. Even adopting the opposite stance is being loyal to the family. For example, someone who grew up with the family message that being frugal with money is important, but instead engages in wild spending is still locked into the family message. Doing the opposite means you must have something to oppose.

Giving the Fear Back

The next step follows quickly behind identifying the voice that taught you to have a particular fear. Now is the time to give that fear back to that individual. You don't have to actually tell the person face to face that you are doing this, so it doesn't matter whether the individual is still alive or not. You can write out the fear, perhaps also writing down why this is no longer relevant to you in your life. You may even want to thank the person for their good intentions in giving you this message—generally adults are trying to protect the children around them, not deliberately sabotage their relationship with money. Then take the paper on which you have written the message, along with the emotion and anything else that's appropriate, and burn it. Or tear it up and flush it down the toilet or bury it beneath an outdoor plant. Do whatever works for you to get rid of the message. It's important to feel the release of both the message and the fear. You may have to do this several times. That doesn't matter. What matters is that you release the fear. Let your partner know what you are doing as well. She or he may want to participate in the releasing ritual.

Embracing Your New Belief

Finally, you're ready to replace the old fear-based message with a new love-based belief. You want your thoughts and feelings associated with money to help both you and your partner get to where you want to be. So make certain your new message will accomplish that. Be careful about the words you choose. Write them down, making certain you understand every word in the new message. Avoid vague terms such as "good" or "a lot" and stick with words that are concrete and have a clear meaning to you.

For example, suppose you have discovered that you've been carrying an old family message that says money is scarce. This has given rise to fear-based anger every time your partner spends money on something you believe is frivolous. The prediction related to this fear says that you will always have to be vigilant and cautious with money, because while you might have enough today, tomorrow could be different. In analyzing your financial situation, you understand that, indeed, you and your partner generate an adequate income. Further, you realize that your fear of not having enough money has fostered a belief that almost everything outside of the basics required to live is frivolous. You can't have fun with the money you do have. And your overly cautious behavior is keeping you from making wise investments that carry more risk than a savings account or certificate of deposit.

Just thinking about changing your message might even trigger fears that by letting go of your old way of seeing money as scarce, you will flip to the other side and become a wild spender who has no savings or investments. Put that imagined fear to rest now. It's just a device to keep you in your current belief. A realistic statement for you might be "Money is plentiful in my life" or "I spend and invest wisely" or "I enjoy my money." The wording must convey the belief you want about your relationship with money. It must also be connected to some love-based emotion such as joy, happiness, or peace. When you repeat your new message to yourself, make sure you can feel the desired emotion along with it.

Once you have completed this process of carefully selecting the wording for your new belief and have connected it to the desired feeling, write the message in as many places as you can think of. Say it as often as you can to yourself, making certain that you feel the desired feelings at the same time. As with all these exercises, ask your partner for help and reinforcement. With diligence, your new message will begin to take the place of the old one, and you will find yourself responding more often from a place of love than fear.

EMBRACING THE POWER OF LOVE

Sometimes people have the mistaken idea that love and love-based emotions are weak, that if they respond to situations from a place of love, then they will be "beaten up" by those individuals who react with fear-based emotions such as anger. This thinking is the opposite of what really happens. If my hold on love is tenuous, I might be pulled into fear by someone who is angry and threatening. But if I am solidly love-based, nothing can move me away from this place of strength. And I will topple fear. Gandhi showed us how strong the power of love can be.

Take a few moments to try an experiment. Stand with your feet about shoulder-width apart and knees bent. Now let yourself feel some familiar fear. You might need to recall a situation to help you do this, but let fear move through your whole body. Notice how you feel. What happens to your muscles? To your breathing? To your heart rate? Would you want to deal with a challenging situation right now? Probably not. Now let the fear go. You might have to shake your body or even take a step away from where you've been standing to help you do this.

Now let yourself feel love, pure unconditional love. Again, it might help to recall a particular person, a pet, or a situation in which you felt thoroughly loved. Give yourself plenty of time to call up this feeling. Let the love move through your whole body. Notice how you feel. What happens to your muscles? To your heart rate? (Studies have shown that blood pressure drops when a person feels loved.) To your breathing? How are these sensations different from being in fear? Most people experience a strength that arises from deep within when they allow themselves to feel love instead of fear. Love is enormously powerful. Too few of us have truly felt that power, however. The last half of this exercise is wonderful to do with your partner. The next time the two of you are dealing with a money issue, you can use this exercise to move into love energy before you begin discussing the issue.

The more accustomed you are to feeling the difference between love and fear throughout your entire body, the easier it will be for you to move out of fear and fear-based reactions and into love and love-based emotions. When you make decisions and solve problems from a basis of love, the resulting actions will likely be solid and will address core issues rather than symptoms. Fear puts an individual into a depowered, victim role that spawns conflict and power struggles. Love nurtures one's self-power, a source of strength accompanied by a knowing that true power means being in charge of oneself and encouraging others to do the same. When two people decide to approach their mutual money issues from this perspective, they can build a positive relationship with money that will enhance their partnership with each other.

Doing the kind of emotional clarifying that we have been talking about in this chapter can certainly serve to bring two people closer together. And that's really the goal here: to assist you and your partner in gaining clarity about emotions tied to money so that you can develop a mutually loving base from which to make money decisions. For our personal growth to continue, we must stay aligned with love. Fear stifles our forward movement while love nurtures it. Perhaps this may be why people so often select partners who will show them their fears—the attraction of opposites. By being in a relationship with someone who reflects back to us our fears and concerns involving money, we have put ourselves into a situation where we have the opportunity to clear out our negative money messages and replace them with constructive beliefs. Both partners must be willing to make the same inner examinations in this process, to be honest with themselves and each other, and to let go of beliefs that don't serve them so that those that do can be embraced. The partnership will only grow and become stronger as a result of this effort.

MOVING FORWARD ▶▶▶▶▶▶▶▶

Our purpose in this chapter is to guide you and your partner in the process of building a positive, love-based relationship with money. Taking the following steps will help you move from fear-based money behaviors to love-based actions:

1. Search for the emotional motivation underlying your money behaviors and determine whether it is fear-based or love-based.

2. Honor your emotions by identifying how your fears have served you.

3. Ask yourself whose voice you hear behind the fear. Who gave you this message?

4. Send your fear-based money beliefs back to the person who gave them to you, releasing their hold on you.

5. Design and embrace a love-based belief to take the place of the fear.

7

MONEY VALUES

"If only I could get Sarah to see things my way, then we wouldn't be having these money problems."

"I don't understand you. Here we are building a business together and you don't want to enjoy any of the money we've worked so hard to earn."

"Look. It's my raise and if I want to buy a new sofa with it, I will. You put plenty of money into our retirement fund for both of us."

Do any of these statements sound familiar? Perhaps you have been on the sending side or the receiving side of one of these messages or something similar. Like the person who made the first statement, we all have a tendency to be so confident in our beliefs that we are certain they are not only right for us, but they are also right for our partner. Furthermore, if we could just get that other person to grasp what we know is true, then we wouldn't be having any difficulties involving money. Like the person quoted in the second example, many owners of new, thriving businesses want to reward themselves for their hard work by using profits to buy new cars and houses while another owner of that same business wants to put the profits back into the business. Finally, we know from numerous surveys that women—like the one who made the third comment—tend to spend money on their children and home improvements while men tend to save more for retirement. What we have in all these instances is a clash of values.

VALUES DEFINED

Our values are the deeply held beliefs that guide our behavior. They drive each of us to make decisions and choices every day of our lives, yet we seldom think about them. They are why one person buys art while another saves for a vacation. This ingrained belief system tells us how much money we need in the bank to feel comfortable. Or it helps us rationalize spending money we don't really have. We acquire our convictions from a variety of sources including family, culture, religion, and the ever-present media. Many of our values are in place before we have developed the rational thinking process to evaluate them in a broader context. In other words, if our parents believed it, chances are we will, too. Or we will engage in a values power struggle and believe the opposite of what we were told and shown. The family genogram you constructed for Chapter 3 gives you a clear picture of the family dynamic from which you derived many of your values.

While family influences are powerful, life experience can facilitate shifts in your value system. What was important to you in your early twenties may be inconsequential to you in your early fifties. You may find yourself rejecting many of your family's values early in adulthood only to embrace some of them later in life. Or as you approach midlife you may hear yourself saying, "been there, done that," regarding some of your money-related values and examining new beliefs that are better suited to who you are now. Such changes in values make exploring these deeply held beliefs with your partner even more important.

Much of the work we have done so far in this book has touched on our values. They give rise to our attitudes toward money. They lie at the root of how we feel about money and about ourselves in relation to money. We may find ourselves having strong emotional responses to what seem to be money-related issues when in fact they are really concerns that challenge our values. Emotionally, people often respond with fear, then anger, when the truth of a belief is challenged. We instinctively want to keep our values intact, since they form much of the solid emotional and psychological ground on which we stand. Too often, these convictions that drive our behaviors and dictate emotions are just below our consciousness. So now we want to focus directly on these deeply held beliefs, bringing them into our awareness.

COMPATIBILITY AND VALUES

Many years ago, when the authors conducted career counseling with individuals, we emphasized that the values held by an employee and those held by the employer (the company, not an individual) must be compatible. If those values are at odds with each other, the employee will be subjected to continuous stress. (It's equally difficult to work for a boss with whom we have values conflicts, but bosses come and go. The organization's values are a integral part of its culture.) It's very hard for us to work effectively in an atmosphere that sends us the message that what is important to us personally has no importance to the organization—and that's the statement made when a values conflict occurs. Sometimes the message is open and obvious, but more often it's subtle, leaving us feeling confused and even dismissed; at the same time we may question our sense of what is right for us. In this work situation, stress dominates. Too often, people fail to realize that a values conflict is at the root of the stress. This kind of job-related problem can be remedied by putting effort into finding an organization with similar values to ours, and vigorously pursuing employment with that company. When we are in a partnership with a values conflict, however, the task is much greater.

Just as people seldom consider values when taking a job, rarely do couples have a "So what, exactly, are your values around money?" conversation prior to making a long-term commitment to each other. This is true whether or not the couple is starting a business together or starting a life together. Values conflicts between two people are usually more challenging to deal with than those that happen between employee and company. When such disagreements arise between individuals, we are often tempted to move into the "I'm right and you're wrong" realm as we struggle to keep our belief systems intact. And when we weave money into this situation, we can, indeed, feel as if we are walking in a minefield. As we have been doing in this book, we want to diffuse the emotion related to our money-related values before attempting to discuss the heart of the issue.

IDENTIFYING VALUES—FAMILY INFLUENCES

There are many methods to help us identify our values. One common money-related approach asks that you look at how you spend your money to determine your values concerning it. Pull out your checkbook and note what you write checks for. Having shelter, food, and clothing is important for most of us, so we pay the mortgage or rent, buy groceries and shoes. When you and your partner review joint spending habits, you can begin to see some common values emerge. Start writing these down, even the obvious ones like food and shelter, so you can both begin to see a picture developing.

At the same time, you may see some potential conflicts. As you make this money values review, ask yourselves, "What value was operating within me when I wrote this check?" or "I spent this money as a result of some underlying belief. What value is this money supporting?" An interesting exercise that drives this question home is to write on the memo line of the check register the value that is behind each expenditure. So if you notice several checks to the local bookstore, you might see that reading for pleasure is important—or perhaps learning about a particular topic is the value that drives the reading. Money spent for birthday gifts could indicate a desire to express love for friends and family through giving something tangible to celebrate a special day. On the other hand, the same spending could reflect your belief that meeting family expectations of gift giving is important, regardless of how you actually feel about the recipient.

Uncovering the values that drive our decisions about and attitudes toward money only begins with the checkbook. A deeper values exploration involves isolating the value that came from a family belief you have been exposed to, putting it into a single word or short phrase, then examining how that conviction manifests itself through your behavior. If you take a closer look at the family messages revealed by the genogram you completed in Chapter 3, you can begin translating those beliefs into values. During one workshop, Sandy told us that she had adopted a family message that as a female she needed to take care of herself because a man may not be around to support her. Independence was an important value to her. In Sandy's life, this value was manifested in having a steady, secure job with substantial savings, separate from her partner's assets. She considered her current situation to be progress since in the past she had been reluctant to enter into any joint financial investments or endeavors with her partner.

BEHAVIORAL DIFFERENCES

But people respond to their values in different ways, sometimes doing the opposite of what we might think they would. In the same workshop, Lois stated that she had received the same family message as Sandy. But for her, it manifested itself very differently. "My belief that a man may not be available to take care of me has unconsciously led me to get involved with men who are financially inept, who cannot hold a steady job, and who are always dependent on me. My notion of independence has meant that I have been the main financial provider in the relationship, the one who outearns my partner, who controls the daily and long-term financial decisions. So my fierce sense of independence hasn't led me into healthy relationships." The value of independence can be expressed in many different ways. What is important in this exploration is to first know what money values you hold, then to understand the ways these beliefs influence your behavior.

BACK TO YOUR GENOGRAM

You already have your genogram with family money messages, so extracting the values you carry that are derived from those beliefs is your next step. Take a look at those messages, and make a list of the values they gave rise to. You might consider things like security, financial dependence or independence, freedom, the external appearance of wealth, or charitable giving. If you write down your beliefs as you uncover them, it will be easier to remember them when you and your partner discuss these influential messages. Writing them also helps to externalize your values and increases the likelihood of your being able to discuss them without emotional distractions.

You may find as you go through your family beliefs that several messages gave rise to and reinforced the same value.

For instance, you may have heard your parents say that working hard is the way to get ahead financially. At the same time, you may have seen them do just that—become increasingly well-off financially as a result of their efforts. Receiving the same admonition verbally and nonverbally makes the resulting value (hard work is the way to financial success) especially deeply entrenched in one's psyche. Conversely, you may discover that an especially strong family message lies at the seat of several values. Hearing the message about hard work from both parents and seeing that message manifested in their financial success can certainly result in the adoption of that belief as a core value, but it may also lead to a belief that gambling is wrong, that being a workaholic is the only way to work, and to many other values that drive behavior. Making these connections between the message and the resulting value can help both you and your partner understand the depth of your emotional commitment to a particular conviction.

Finally, ask yourself how your behaviors are linked to these values, keeping in mind that a single value can give rise to many different behaviors. For example, valuing financial security may mean always making sure you have enough money to pay the mortgage or rent. It may also lead you to having a certain amount of money in the bank. For some people having multiple investments means security, while others want their cash more accessible. Sticking with the same employer means security to many individuals, even if the salary might be higher with another, less stable, organization. Others find safety in constantly learning and changing, even when this means switching jobs and careers; their security comes from an internal sense rather than from external events. One of the revelations you and your partner may have during this examination is that while you may share the same value, its meaning and consequently how it affects your behavior may be very different.

SEEING YOUR VALUES

An excellent way to graphically see how your behaviors are linked to your values is to construct a pie chart that reflects what you have learned about yourself and your money values so far. You and your partner can create individual charts, then compare them for similarities and differences. The idea here is to create a visual representation

of the equation: Values + Behaviors = Individual Expenditures. Sometimes one picture is worth a thousand words, as the saying goes. To
make this suggested exercise easier, focus on four major categories
of money behaviors: spending (including mortgage, food, loan payments, etc.), saving/investing, giving, and playing (entertainment).
Now with the information you have about your behaviors in each
of these areas, fill in a circle with the percentage of your total income
that you devote to each area. Remember, you are each creating a
pie for your income, so even if you are sharing expenses equally, if
your incomes are different, your individual charts will look very different.

Your pie chart might look something like this:

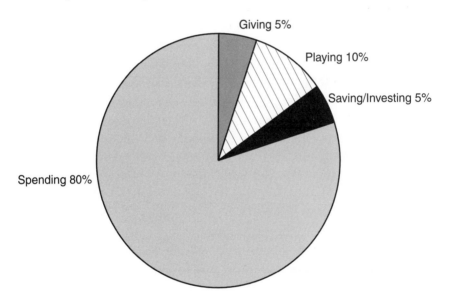

This pie ought to represent the percentage of your total income
you actually put into each of these areas. If it's helpful, you may
want to break down these segments into more detail. Once both
you and your partner have drawn your money pies, you're ready to
discuss what you have each learned about yourselves from this process. Illustrating expenditures in this way is another activity that
helps you to detach the emotion from the behavior, making your
behaviors and the reasons behind them easier to discuss.

Discussing your Chart

As with all these partner meetings, each needs to refrain from judging or criticizing the other's behavior. Agree before starting your values discussion whether or not you want to give each other feedback. On the plus side, because you know each other well, you may see ways your partner expresses underlying values that she or he doesn't see. On the minus side, if the other's responses are incorrectly handled, the discussion can quickly degenerate into an argument. The feedback issue can be managed in several ways. You might both agree to forego any input from the other and focus on listening to what each individual has learned about him- or herself. You can set another time for listening to what your partner has observed about your value-related money behaviors.

If you both decide to give each other feedback during this initial discussion, some guidelines can help keep the emphasis on sharing information and away from accusing. A major challenge is for each person to listen fully to the other while resisting the temptation to formulate thoughts, remember examples of behaviors, and wrestle with emotions. In other words, listen rather than waiting to talk.

Before you tell your partner about your perceptions, ask permission to provide feedback regarding behaviors that might be connected to the value. This will both increase the likelihood that you will be heard and lessen the chance that your partner will feel as if she or he has to go on the defensive. While you share your impressions of your partner's behaviors, be willing to be wrong. If your partner doesn't understand the connection between a stated value and your assessment of a related behavior and you can't make your point, then let it go. There may not be a connection, or your partner may not be ready to grasp it. The goal of this values and behaviors discussion is to create a more complete picture of money-related issues for you and your partner and to increase your understanding of the root causes of your various money behaviors.

IDENTIFYING VALUES—RELIGION'S INFLUENCE

As mentioned earlier, while our values system originates within our families, they aren't our only source. Religion sends us powerful directives about money. Probably the best known of these messages is "Money is the root of all evil." The actual quote is "The love of money is the root of all evil," an entirely different message that can lead to a much healthier view of money than believing it to be the underlying cause of everything evil. The values derived from these two messages are very different. The first version of this belief is quite common in organized religions. At the same time members are expected to give money to sustain the religious organization, its buildings, and its leaders. Thus a money-related conflict is born— this religion is founded on love, yet it is sustained by something that is the root of all evil.

Another religion-based message that can give rise to a contradiction in values is reflected in the belief "It is easier for a camel to pass through the eye of a needle than for a rich man to enter the kingdom of heaven." How does someone with an abundance of money reconcile his or her financial worth with this religious value? Or suppose I embrace this belief, yet I see people who donate large sums of money to religions receiving praise for their financial contributions and being treated like a "good guy." The subtle message that can come through in this situation is that, unlike the rich man in the Biblical quote, this wealthy individual is okay and will undoubtedly get into heaven since he has done so much good with his money. This is another confusing dilemma to grapple with as we try to form and clarify our internal values system regarding money.

If you were brought up as part of an organized religion, what direct and indirect messages did you receive regarding money? Which ones made sense to you and which held contradictions? Write down as many of these messages as you can think of along with the associated values.

IDENTIFYING VALUES—CULTURAL INFLUENCES

In this process of exploration, you may discover that several messages from differing sources led you to the same value. You probably will find you received many more messages than you have values, since we tend to associate similar messages and distill them into a single belief. After you have looked at family and religion, ask yourself what values you derived from your culture.

Culturally connected messages are often delivered via the media in newscasts, sitcoms, game shows, and the all-pervasive advertising. Ads attempt to hook into our existing values or to convince us to adopt new values. (One area of significant debate is whether advertisers actually instill certain values in their audience or just play off existing values.) Chapter 4—Cultural Messages gave you a good idea of what we're talking about here.

What values have you adopted that are shared by your culture? As you have done with the other messages you've received, search out the beliefs you have developed from the messages you pay attention to. These may be very different from your partner's.

For instance, automobile manufacturers try to appeal to various values held by consumers. Many people in the United States hold the value that bigger is better. So U.S. auto companies are known for building many models of large cars, trucks, vans, and recreational vehicles and SUVs. The ads for these vehicles emphasize size and power over everything else. However, people who value economy in a vehicle will be unimpressed with large machines that have low miles-per-gallon ratings. They will opt for fuel-efficient, smaller cars. When someone who values size in a vehicle is in a relationship with someone who values economy and they try to buy a car together, some conflicts are likely. When both individuals are aware of what their values are and how they are manifested in the car-buying arena, the chances for conflict are much lower and the likelihood of pre-purchase compromise is much greater.

Uncovering the values that drive your behaviors is not the simple task it may have initially appeared to be. But the effort pays off in a clearer understanding of where your decisions and emotions concerning money originate, putting you in conscious control of your money-related behaviors and enhancing your understanding of the origins of many of the money conflicts between you and your partner. You may be able to see where the same value gives rise to differing behaviors. Perhaps the two of you have more money-related values in common than you realized. Knowing what we share gives us a place to begin building core values for the relationship and a foundation from which we can resolve or reconcile problems arising from dissimilar values.

SORTING OUT YOUR VALUES

At this point you and your partner can probably make a list of your shared money values, along with the behaviors and outcomes you want from them. For example, suppose you both share the value of a financially independent retirement. Leaping ahead to the outcome, this means that as a couple you will want to be able to generate a certain amount of income from investments and retirement accounts to maintain a particular standard of living after you have both stopped working. Agreeing on the numbers involved—how much income and how much in various investments—translates into actions around how much money gets put into mutual retirement accounts now. Meeting these goals may mean taking a less expensive vacation or making other budgetary adjustments.

As long as you both embrace the same value, and its desired outcome, the two of you will support the behaviors necessary to realize it, a critical aspect of successfully achieving your goal. No one feels deprived by the shorter vacation, for example. There's no sabotage by breaking the budget, no overspending by buying oneself or the other an inordinately expensive gift. Openly supporting agreed-upon values takes away power struggles that can happen as a result of values conflicts.

PRIORITIZING YOUR VALUES

Because we do generally have multiple values and we need to know how these values relate in terms of their importance, we need to prioritize them. (If you only have a few items on your individual values list, you probably don't need to do this.) If you and your partner do the following activity at the same time, then there's a far greater likelihood that you both will actually rank your values in order of priority. You can motivate each other. Sometimes people try to cut corners when prioritizing by looking at the entire list and attempting to pick out the most important item, then the next most important, and on down the line. This approach is usually overwhelming—it's too much to compare everything on the list with everything else on the list and pick out number one, then number two, and so on. We are going to suggest a system that allows you to prioritize by only having to compare two items at a time.

To begin, each of you should simply number your own list of values. Right now, the order doesn't matter. Focusing first on values numbered one and two, ask yourself which one is more important. Then put a mark beside your response. Next compare number one and number three, again asking yourself which is more important and marking off your choice. Continue on through your list in that manner, comparing the number one value to each one below it and marking your response. When you reach the last value on the list, go back to your number two value and compare it to number three, and so on, again working your way down the list comparing only two values at a time. Repeat this process until each value has been compared to every other value. Your list might look something like this:

1. Immediate financial security x x x x

2. Paying for the children's higher education x x x

3. Independence x

4. Having nice things x

5. Charitable giving x

Meanwhile, your partner's list might look like this:

1. Financial independence x x

2. Supporting my family x x

3. Enjoying my money x

4. Showing my success

Now count your marks and rewrite your list in order of importance, according to your results. If you have a tie, just compare the two items again and make your choice. You may find that one or more items have no mark beside them. When this happens, you find out that these values, while they exist for you, are not as important as you thought they were. This is good information and it is exactly what prioritizing values shows—what is really important. Discuss your list with your partner, looking for areas of agreement—the challenges will be obvious. As always, make certain you understand how these values manifest themselves in behaviors. In discussing each other's money values, areas of differing behaviors may come to light. If you each avoid judging and instead seek to understand, you will make significant progress toward resolving areas of conflict.

Suppose security has a high value for you, manifesting itself in your desire to have a large savings account. On the other hand, your partner may value the freedom to spend that having a steady income can give people. So your partner enjoys spending while you strive to save. Once you both understand the values underlying the behaviors, then you can begin talking objectively about how your individual beliefs are at odds with each other rather than getting caught up in the emotions tied to the behaviors. You can also begin exploring areas where you can both support the other's values. By examining the reality of your financial situation, you may realize that you don't need as much money in the bank as you thought you did. You may be able to enjoy your money more by loosening the purse strings a bit. You're not attempting to change the importance that financial security has for you, you're just shifting your behavior to reflect what may be a more realistic way of maintaining that value—and allowing yourself to have some fun with the money you earn.

Conversely, you and your partner can spend cooperatively within agreed-upon guidelines that accommodate both values. This new standard might mean that your partner no longer has as much money to spend on fun, but it will also mean that when he or she does act on this value, it won't evoke your fears about your financial security. So you have both shifted your behaviors to a more realistic position that reflects your current financial situation and honors each other's values. People are more likely to alter behaviors than they are to change values.

PRIORITIZING YOUR SHARED VALUES

Now you're ready to move on to the values you and your partner share. Take another look at this list to make certain it accurately reflects your shared values. Next, prioritize this list individually and then exchange what you have done with your partner. It's always a good idea for couples to know which of their money values comes first. You may share the value of saving for a vacation each year and putting money aside for retirement. But which one comes first? And how much of your income ought to go into each account? This is where prioritizing helps clarify things. Sometimes both partners place almost the same importance on the values; sometimes their priorities are reversed. In the latter case you may want to clarify what you each mean by the value, and you'll also need to do some negotiating. Certainly the two people who created the individual lists in the above example have some negotiating to do before developing a mutually agreed-upon list.

Arriving at a prioritized money-values list that you both support is critical to your success as a couple with shared money interests. It forms the foundation for all your money-related decisions. When working toward a joint prioritized money-values list, don't be tempted to agree to something that you don't really support. You will soon find yourself resentful of the way money is being used to fulfill that value, and eventually you will consciously or unconsciously find ways to sabotage your money plan. Realize also that the two of you may not be able to come up with an agreed-upon list as a result of one discussion. It may take several talks, lots of negotiating, and some passage of time, although hopefully not too much time.

ANOTHER PIE

Now is the time for the two of you to create a joint-expenditure pie. Looking at what you have learned about your shared and individual values, draw your pie with the percentages of total income you jointly devote to general spending, saving/investing, giving, and playing. While it might seem that this pie will be the same as your individual chart, that's not necessarily the case. When couples do not have joint accounts or do not mix their money, this illustration will be very different from the individual charts. This is especially true among gay and lesbian couples, who often keep totally separate accounts and simply share in paying monthly bills. This type of arrangement means that the two people seldom have a shared vision for the role of money in their relationship. They treat money almost as if it were irrelevant. We know otherwise. So this pie chart representation of how the combined incomes are spent is very revealing. When a couple has no shared money goals except basic expenses, the resulting pie chart may only show the percentage of combined income that goes to spending. The rest of the pie may be blank. While this arrangement can be healthy for some couples, others may feel the hole in the relationship represented by the hole in the chart.

Once you have completed the pie chart showing actual expenditures, the two of you can create your ideal chart, depicting how you would both like to allocate your shared expenditures. Incorporating your shared values list into the reality of your income gives you a picture of what you would both like to attain. We encourage couples to hang this ideal chart where they can see it frequently. Business partners may want to each have one to hang in their respective offices. The bathroom mirror might be appropriate for couples living together. This semipublic display also helps to bring money and its related issues out of the closet.

THE REWARDS

The results of this thorough approach are well worth the effort. You and your partner are forming the solid groundwork for a thriving relationship with money that will last your entire time together. And we know that having this kind of agreement on money values greatly enhances the likelihood of your being together a very long time, whether you are in a marriage, committed relationship, or business.

With regard to a business, building shared money values at the outset results in a clearer corporate culture when it comes to money. If business partners are at odds with their money values, their company will send conflicting messages about money to their employees and to their customers. A precise statement of values supported by the partners ought to appear in every business plan and be available to every employee.

THE COOPERATIVE APPROACH

We are continually encouraging couples to take a cooperative approach to understanding and honoring each other's values because it is vital to having a healthy relationship with each other and with money. People are much less likely to get carried away emotionally when dealing with someone else's troublesome behaviors if the underlying value is understood. If, for example, you are a security-conscious saver dealing with your partner's happy spending, you can both take a more thorough approach to resolving the difficulty when his or her spending upsets you. First, you recognize that the spending has triggered your fears concerning financial security. A quick analysis of your financial situation can go a long way toward giving you some realistic information that tells you whether or not your fears are grounded in reality. Next, ask yourself exactly what your partner did—overspend the agreed-upon budget, indulge in spending without consulting you, or in some other way violate agreements you have both made with each other? Isolating the specific behavior helps you to clarify what happened and aids you in staying away from harmful generalizations such as "You don't care about this relationship." Your partner also needs to conduct a similar self-examination about his or her spending behavior and underlying motives.

Now you are ready to address the situation with each other. Clear communication means stating how you felt as a result of the spending. For example: "I'm angry that you spent more than our budget allowed" or "We agreed that we would both make decisions about spending this amount of money. I'm hurt that you violated our agreement." While this language may sound contrived because we don't normally talk this way, it plainly states your reaction and the behavior involved. It opens the door to communicating further. An angry or hurt reaction involving blaming, yelling, or pouting shuts down communication. Such a reaction might be "You spent money we don't have. I knew you wouldn't honor our agreement. What are you trying to do to me?" In response, your partner will probably find it impossible to remember to focus on the underlying values and will instead go into a defensive posture. This reaction may result in more yelling in defense of his or her behavior. Or it may lead to placating behavior that eventually results in resentment; the animosity gets stifled but eventually finds its way out, possibly manifesting itself in another spending spree.

A Healthy Resolution

Let's go back to what is likely to happen when both partners strive to keep communication open by stating their feelings, getting to the core of what is happening by talking about the values involved, and staying away from blaming and accusatory language. By focusing on a prior agreement regarding saving and spending, you can both figure out what led to your partner's overspending. He or she now has the opportunity to examine negative behaviors that may be associated with the money-is-fun value. Once this level of understanding is reached, the two of you can explore how to rectify what has happened. If the object of the expense is returnable, that may be the solution. (Incidentally, the return is your partner's responsibility, not yours.) Another solution would be to decrease or eliminate the "fun money" in the budget for several weeks or until the amount overspent is made up.

It's important that you both work through this challenge together and agree on a solution acceptable to both. If either of you feels deprived or resents the solution, those feelings will gain expression in another destructive behavior sooner or later. For example, if you feel a trust has been violated and the resolution you and your partner come up with doesn't heal that wound, you may very well take on a parental role in dictating the entire budget. Neither of you can then support your shared values. When you both stay focused on the values you want to make manifest in your relationship, then you can turn conflicts into win-win situations.

Approaching money conflicts with clarity about the values underlying our behaviors is extremely important to a healthy relationship. It takes constant vigilance at first, and the process of working out difficulties may initially feel awkward and time-consuming. But eventually this new way of coping with money challenges will mean a smoother and healthier relationship between the two of you and your money.

MOVING FORWARD ▶ ▶ ▶ ▶ ▶ ▶ ▶ ▶

This chapter aims to help you clarify the key to many of your money behaviors—your values. By proceeding through the following summary of activities, you and your partner will identify your individual and shared values, a critical process for developing a more positive relationship with each other and with money.

1. Conduct a money-values review with your partner, looking for similarities and differences.
2. Refer to your genogram to isolate family values.
3. Connect your values with your behaviors.
4. Construct a pie chart that shows your actual expenditures and compare it to your values.
5. Have an open, nonjudgmental discussion about what you have each discovered, using your pie chart and genograms as focal points.
6. Create a list of your individual and shared values and prioritize each list.
7. Draw a joint-expenditure pie chart, then an ideal joint-expenditure pie chart.

8

MONEY AND SECRECY

We are only as sick as the secrets we keep, or so the saying goes. If this is true, then when it comes to money, many of us must surely be on the critical list. The topic of money is so laden with prohibitions that we are acutely uncomfortable discussing it with casual acquaintances, let alone our nearest and dearest. Money has long been a taboo topic in our society. We will tell friends intimate details of our latest medical procedure, discuss a partner's infidelity, enumerate our struggles with our children, but when it comes to money, our lips are sealed. So we squirm when discussing our salary or telling a friend the price of our new car or how much we are spending to send our children to that private school. Even our etiquette books tell us that money is not a proper subject for general conversation.

In relationships this prohibition against talking about money is further complicated by an emotional overlay. Because we can't talk about money, it gains an inordinate amount of power. Money has a way of becoming so much more than just money. It can be a method of measuring ourselves, a way to show or withhold love, a means to punish or reward behavior, a reason to keep or end a relationship. And usually it can be these things without anybody saying a word about money or discussing what is really going on. We learn to keep secrets—secrets that have the power to do major damage to our relationships. Let's look at some of the secrets we keep about money.

SPENDING SECRETS

"I know I promised Paula that we would economize on groceries, but I just couldn't resist buying those gourmet sauces. If I slip them into the cupboard among what is already there, she will probably never notice," said Kelly, a 48-year-old real estate broker, with a slightly embarrassed grin.

"If my parents know I spent my allowance on clothes again, they'll have a fit," confided Mira, a 20-year-old college student. "So I'll tell them I had to buy more books for my art class. They'll never know the difference. And I did need those shoes."

"I buy things for the kids and then make them promise not to tell their father," admitted Mollie, a 32-year-old mother of three. "He blows up if I spend on stuff he considers nonessential. He is such a tightwad, this is the only way I can get what we need."

"I really need that chip for my computer," said Ted, a 40-year-old office manager. "If I tell my wife though, she'll just say it's frivolous. It's easier to say nothing for now and hope she doesn't discover the check that I wrote."

"I'm going to pay for part of this in cash and the rest I'll put on my credit card," Stacey said to her hair stylist. "That way my husband won't fuss at me for spending so much."

These people share a common behavior—they spend and then don't tell a partner or parent what they have done. The surface reasons *why* they believe they can't tell about their spending vary. Kelly and Paula are struggling financially and have agreed to watch their budget. Mira chronically overspends her allowance and her parents want her to learn to be more frugal. Mollie is married to a miserly type of guy who resists spending for anything but what *he* considers important. Ted's wife thinks computers are a colossal waste of time and money, so anything Ted spends would be unnecessary in her view. Stacey's husband thinks she spends too much on her hair; she disagrees, so she just keeps the amount a secret. All of these people have reasons for their secret keeping that make sense to them and sound logical on the surface. But secrets damage relationships.

Secret keeping about spending is common. A recent poll reported in the August 2001 issue of the *Reader's Digest* revealed that 48 percent of spouses reported fudging on the real price of something they had bought.[1] Some of the secrets are minor, some are not. Generally however, keeping secrets about spending usually indicates a relationship imbalance. So when secrets are kept, we have to look beneath the behaviors to understand what is really going on. Let's look at our five examples and see what else might be happening.

Kelly

Kelly is bright and attractive and loves her career as a real estate broker. Unfortunately for Kelly, every time the economy takes a dip, so does her income. Paula, on the other hand, owns and manages an employment agency that supplies temporary workers for some of the most successful businesses in their city. Paula's income has been growing steadily as her agency takes hold and gains a following. Because of the need for temporary employees in their city, and Paula's skills at hiring competent employees, her business will continue to grow and prosper. Kelly's extravagances are really attempts to equalize the relationship. Kelly is a little jealous of Paula's success, although admitting it was very difficult for her. By spending on things Paula didn't want her to, Kelly could feel more equal to Paula.

Mira

Mira's parents live in another state and are quite wealthy. They are happy to supply Mira with the means to pursue her college degree and are more than generous in giving Mira an allowance. The problem is that Mira can never stay within her means. In talking this over with her college counselor, Mira realized that her secret spending is really the result of anger. She wants her parents to care about what she is doing in school, not just send money. Her secret spending is a way of getting back at them for their lack of interest in her studies.

Mollie

Mollie gave up her teaching career to stay home with the couple's three children. Initially she thought this was a good bargain, but after about a year she finds that she resents not having money that she earned. An additional problem is that her husband is extremely frugal, so anything Mollie spends is questioned and must be justified to him. She feels powerless in the relationship and finds that secret spending is one way she can feel a little bit of control. Spending also helps to keep her mind off her concerns about putting her career on hold to be a stay-at-home mom.

Ted

Ted genuinely likes computers and other technical gadgets. If it is new, he wants it. His secret spending came from a lack of assertiveness. He wants to discuss his needs with his wife, but is afraid of her anger. His secret spending is a way of passively avoiding anger, either imagined or real.

Stacey

Stacey and her husband have some major disagreements over how to spend the money they have. Stacey feels that her weekly stylist's appointment is a necessity, given that her job as a bank teller constantly places her in the public eye. Her husband thinks Stacey spends too much on personal care and wants her to cut down on the amount she pays out each month. They have never really taken the time to talk about how to meet their needs cooperatively, so the secret spending is a way for Stacey to get what she wants without a confrontation.

SECRET SPENDING—A MEANS TO AN END

All of these examples demonstrate that secret spending usually is not about the item purchased. It is only a means to an end. This practice probably began when money first replaced bartering as means of exchange and has continued ever since. It isn't the money that is at issue here, it is an unmet need. This unmet need is coupled with a lack of trust and mutual goals. In order for a relationship to be healthy, honesty and shared goals need to exist. This cannot happen in the presence of secrets. One way to overcome the need for secrecy is to take a hard look at the real issue. If you are a secret spender, ask yourself:

What is really going on here?

What need is unmet?

What am I trying to fix?

Where is the imbalance in this relationship?

The answers to these questions will give you some tools to move past secret spending and open the way to a more balanced relationship.

INFIDELITY—THE ULTIMATE SECRET SPENDING

Another, more serious, variation on the secret spending theme comes when one partner uses money to support an illicit affair. The partner may be secretly maintaining a separate residence where the adulterous couple can meet, or paying the living expenses of the lover, or even supporting a second family. Secret spending may be used to buy trips, expensive gifts, pricey lunches, or dinners. This type of spending is the most hurtful type of secret spending. Usually the deceived partner is oblivious to what is happening, and when the secret spending is discovered, is deeply wounded. Not only was the partner seeing someone else, but the couple's funds were diverted to support the relationship. What the dishonest partner is really saying is something like, "This relationship is not working for me, and I don't want to deal with it directly. Instead, I'll do something underhanded to get my needs met." According to psychologist Cloé Madanes, "When affairs are tied to financial loss or to deception about money, the marriage almost inevitably ends with a separation."[2]

If your money secrets fall into this category, you will probably find that you need to work with a therapist to help you understand what is happening with you. And you will need help in extricating yourself from the situation and taking steps so that it is not repeated.

EARNING SECRETS

Partners also keep secrets about how much money they earn. In the groups we've lead and the individual counseling we have done, we hear a repeated refrain, "I can't tell him/her how much I make. It would be too upsetting." We have already discussed the problems that occur when one partner outearns the other. Many times this is the reason for the secrecy—one partner's self-esteem is threatened by being outearned, so a conspiracy of protective silence is maintained. This pattern is usually seen when the female earns more than the male, but can happen in any relationship when money and self-worth are tightly bound. Healthy couples will want to move past this pattern and forge a definition of worth that does not include money.

Secrets may be kept about how much money is earned when the primary wage earner sees money as a power issue. In this case, not disclosing the amount of income keeps the partner off-balance and fearful, and gives the wage-earning partner power. We discuss money and power in Chapter 9. If this dynamic is operating in your relationship, reading that chapter may help you move toward a more equitable relationship.

Our belief is that couples who want their relationship to thrive will have an honest exchange about how much money each brings to the partnership. We do recognize, however, that sometimes couples agree not to disclose the amount of their earnings. If this is an agreement and both parties are comfortable with the arrangement, then clearly it is working for that particular couple. In one instance, an agreement to keep a secret actually saved a relationship. Here is how that worked:

Amy and Jake were both in a second marriage. Jake's first wife had never worked outside the home, so Jake felt strongly about meeting his spousal-support obligations. Amy resented the support payments bitterly and thought Jake's ex-wife should just get a job and leave them alone. Their marriage could have broken up over this issue, and ironically, an agreed-upon secret saved them. They solved their problem by agreeing to a budget arrangement in which both partners contributed a set amount to their joint account. Whatever was left over after joint obligations were met was considered discretionary money, to be spent as each saw fit. Amy agreed not to ask the amount of support money Jake was sending his first wife, and Jake agreed not to discuss it. In this way, Jake could still send the spousal-support payments he saw as his obligation, and Amy could be left out of the whole process. They never discussed the matter and their relationship held together.

We do emphasize that the way Jake and Amy handled their issue was the exception rather than the rule. They loved each other and developed an unorthodox solution to a touchy problem. They agreed to have a secret. Generally, being honest is the best policy unless the couple has a good reason for acting otherwise.

Other families keep secrets about the total amount of their household income. Frequently, parents are reluctant to tell their children exactly what they earn. The fear is that the children will then have unrealistic expectations about what the family can and cannot do. We have found that this usually doesn't happen. When handled correctly, information about income can be a valuable part of the child's financial education. To a child, a yearly income of $40,000 can sound like vast wealth. It might seem otherwise if the parents take the opportunity to teach the child about how the family budget works and even include the child in family budget meetings. As we discuss in Chapter 15, we believe that children need financial education. Knowing how much money the family has can help children learn about finances and increase their confidence about handling their own money. By being open about money, parents can set a powerful example for their children.

SECRET SAVING

Sometimes, secrets about saving accounts occur for benign or even positive reasons. The classic story about an immigrant family told in *I Remember Mama* is just such an example. In the book and later the movie, the children always felt safe because, whenever there was a financial crisis, their mother reassured them by saying she could go to her bank account if things really got bad. Knowledge of this safety net was comforting to the children. When problems were solved without drawing on Mama's account, the children would breathe a sigh of relief. The bank account was still there! As an adult, the author of the book was amazed to learn that the bank account, which had provided such reassurance in scary times, never existed. Mama believed that knowing the family's real financial condition would be frightening for the children, so she gave them confidence by helping them feel secure about money. And because this confidence allowed the family to work together to solve problems, the strategy apparently worked.

Not many money secrets are this helpful. Couples who keep saving secrets usually have less helpful motivations. Sometimes couples have saving accounts that they keep secret from each other. Here is such an example involving one couple we know.

> Audrey and Lou had been married for 20 years when Audrey resumed her teaching career. She began to hold back some money from each paycheck, depositing it into an account her husband had no idea existed. Eventually she began using the money to make some investments, which turned out to be quite lucrative. Her secret account had grown to a respectable amount, and it signified security to her, she told us. When we asked her why she believed she needed to do this, her response was telling. "He had several affairs years ago and since then I have never felt safe with him. I need to be able to take care of myself. Besides, I figure this is payback for him. What he doesn't know now makes me feel better about what I didn't know then!"

Like secret spending, the practice of secret saving usually indicates that something is out of balance in the relationship. The person who keeps the secret needs the reassurance of having money set aside or maybe is holding on to anger over some past event in the relationship. Whatever the reason, we encourage you to look at the secrets that you keep and discover what lies beneath them. This information can be an important clue to the dynamics in your relationship and may enable you to make some positive changes in the way you deal with your partner.

SECRET DEBTS
Secrets about debts can also keep couples from having an open relationship as far as money is concerned. Sometimes partners enter relationships with debts they do not disclose. Other times the debts

may be accumulated after the relationship starts. Either way, such secrets are bound to cause problems. By their very nature, secret debts result from a lack of trust in the partner. And they attest to the fact that the person in debt has something to hide.

Sometimes secret debts can indicate out-of-control spending habits. If this is the case, the couple needs to sit down and agree on a way to bring spending under control. Honest communication and re-establishment of trust are vital to this process. In many communities, debt counseling is available at little or no cost; this may be another necessary step. Once the spending issues are in check, the couple can begin to work on other money issues in the relationship.

Debts may be kept secret to cover an addiction such as gambling or drinking. Sometimes they hide a compulsive shopping addiction. In the case of an addiction, the person with the secret debts needs to get help for that problem before tackling the money issues in the relationship. There are many qualified therapists who deal with addictions and can be helpful in this situation. There are also Twelve-Step groups that provide support and information about changing such behaviors. The partners can both benefit from getting in a group to support and guide them while they work their way out of the addictive behaviors. Once this is done, they can work on rebuilding the relationship.

SECRETS FROM THE GRAVE

Some family secrets come to light only after a death in the family. A recent example of this type of secret is illustrated by a court case concerning the estate of the well-known journalist Charles Kuralt. Famous for his folksy manner and his CBS series *On the Road*, Kuralt had apparently led a double life for 29 years, supporting another woman and a second family. When Kuralt died at age 62, the woman sued to gain possession of a Montana retreat the two had shared. Reportedly, the property had been promised to her by Kuralt, but he died before he could put his promise in writing. As the case unfolded, details about the secret life emerged, leaving Kuralt's wife, family, friends, and fans aghast.[3]

Other family secrets may be less spectacular but can be equally hurtful. "I never realized how clearly my grandmother preferred my brother to me until we learned the contents of the will," Laura said. "My brother Tyler got all of Grandmother's stocks, the land she owned, plus a sizable sum of money. I got her diamond ring, which is lovely, but really can't compare to what Tyler received. I knew she adored Tyler. He was the only grandson, so Grandmother saw him as important in carrying on the family line. Still, I was flabbergasted by the inequity of it all. And she never gave any indication of what she was going to do. Tyler was as surprised as I was when this all came out. I am so hurt that it is hard for me to have positive memories of her."

In other families, an inheritance can be used to reward or punish a family member. And this treatment often comes as a surprise because of the secret keeping that surrounded it. Anthony, for example, did not find out until after his mother's death just how angry she was that he had married outside the family religion and raised their children in his wife's faith. His mother left her entire estate to the church. He received nothing. "It wasn't the money," he told us. "I make a good salary and am fine without it. What really hurt was that she never discussed her feelings. I just didn't realize that she had been holding on to so much anger for so long."

Sometimes when there is a death, the family finds out that the money they counted on is no longer there. "James always told me not to worry about money," said Amanda, a 70-year-old widow. "He said he had it all taken care of. But he had borrowed against his life insurance to invest in a business that failed, so the insurance is gone. He thought he would be around long enough to pay it back, but it just didn't work out that way. I don't know what I'll do now."

These types of secrets are probably the most difficult to handle. The secret keeper is gone, and the survivors have little recourse. All they can do is deal with their feelings and move on. But secrets leave a scar. And frequently the secret becomes the most powerful recollection of the deceased, wiping out other more positive memories.

BREAKING FREE FROM SECRETS

Secret keeping is damaging. There is no doubt about it. Couples keep secrets for a variety of reasons, but only when secret keeping is mutually agreed upon can it be beneficial to a relationship. Breaking free of secret keeping takes a commitment to honesty. It also requires hard work. If you and your partner are ready to move away from secret keeping, here are some steps for you to follow.

1. **Go to the source.** The first step in changing this pattern is to understand where it comes from. We recommend that you go back to your genogram and determine if there have been any secrets in your family of origin. Make note of any secrets you uncover. Ask yourself:

   Who were the secret keepers and what were the secrets about?

   How do the secrets affect you today?

   What do you want to do differently?

2. **Do a thorough self-examination.** Spend some time by yourself thinking about your relationship. Ask yourself:

   What are your secrets really about? Are they an indicator of some need that is not being met? If so, what is it?

   Do your secrets stifle some unexpressed anger? What do you really need to talk about with your partner?

   Are your secrets an expression of some inequality in your relationship? What do you need to do to bring it back into balance?

   What can you do instead of keeping secrets?

3. **Let go of secrets.** Have a frank discussion with your partner in which you both resolve to let go of any secrets you have been holding. This, too, will require an atmosphere of trust and loving support. But assuming you are both committed to maintaining a healthy relationship, this will be a powerful step in clearing the air. As with all the discussions we have recommended in the book, you need to pick a time when you will be uninterrupted and can speak freely. If the discussion begins to get emotional, call for a time-out so you each can regroup and think clearly. Be aware that this step may take several sessions, so keep at it until you both are comfortable with what has been brought up. When you have said all that needs to be said, make a promise to each other to let go of the past. That

means that neither of you will use old mistakes as a weapon against the other, and that both of you will assume that new behaviors begin now.

4. **Make a new plan.** Finally, make a commitment to keep your relationship secret-free. You have struggled to reach this point. You have done an honest self-examination and revealed your secrets to your partner. You have been heard and accepted. The payoff is that you will probably experience a great feeling of relief. Keeping secrets is hard work, and a heavy burden has been lifted. You can now move into a relationship based on trust and honesty.

5. **Reward yourselves.** You have completed a very important task—letting go of secrets. This process is painful and exhausting. You deserve a reward for sticking with it to the end. We recommend you allow yourselves some "couple time" to celebrate with an activity you both enjoy. Take a walk, go out for ice cream, see a movie, visit a museum. By spending time together you are solidifying your relationship and affirming your commitment as a couple.

MOVING FORWARD ▶▶▶▶▶▶▶▶▶

This chapter has examined different types of money secrets and illustrated the damage such secrets can cause in a relationship. You may have identified some areas in which you would like to make changes. We encourage you to begin the process immediately. Letting go of money secrets is a liberating experience. By doing so, you acknowledge your commitment to your partner and your relationship. You move your relationship to a healthier place where you can experience new levels of trust and mutuality.

Here are some steps you can take to begin the process of letting go of secrets.

1. List any money secrets you have identified from your family of origin.

2. List any money secrets you see in your current relationship.

3. Pick one area in which you want to see change.

4. Develop an action plan for dealing honestly with your partner.

5. Write your action plan on paper and post it where you can see it frequently.

6. Enlist your partner's support in sticking to your action plan. Agree upon a reward to encourage continued growth.

9

THE POWER DIFFERENTIAL

E ntire books are written on the power struggles in relationships, discussing their overt and covert origins, ways to resolve them, and their potential destructiveness. A major reason underlying the breakup of many marriages and other primary relationships can be found in power conflicts involving money. Likewise, people in business partnerships often find themselves facing emotionally charged money issues that can easily be manifested in power conflicts. This all-important dynamic never makes it into the business plan.

At its simplest, a power struggle between two people means one is trying to control the other, to get the other to behave in a particular way, or to take responsibility for some event that is not really his or her fault. When we become caught up in this kind of conflict, we can quickly become entrenched in the rightness of our individual beliefs, convinced that no problem would exist if things were done our way.

UNDERSTANDING MOTIVATIONS

Some people experience every interaction with their partner as a power struggle. These people view relationships from the perspective of needing to be in control, and they experience all encounters as a potential threat to that control. Such a person may or may not have this attitude with anyone else, but he or she does have it in intimate relationships. Attempts to engage in meaningful communication to gain clarity about issues, especially those that have a strong emotional tie, are experienced as threats to this person's sense of power in the relationship. Thus he or she may lash out with what seems to be an inappropriate response to the partner's attempts to talk something out. This individual will do whatever it takes to maintain his or her sense of being in control, even becoming abusive.

The other way of viewing relationships is that they are founded on mutuality, on trust and openness and support for each partner's growth and maturation. Communication in this dynamic is viewed as a means of enhancing understanding and furthering the intimacy between two people. Differences are respected. Consensus is the key to resolving disagreements and misunderstandings in this type of relationship. The individual who embraces this perspective is usually baffled by the person who believes partnerships are vehicles for asserting power over another. When these two get together, one becomes the abuser and the other the victim. They are in a constant struggle, one trying to keep control and the other mistakenly believing that if she or he communicates clearly, the other will see the light. Unfortunately, the dynamic these two are caught in will only cease being a struggle when each understands the reality embraced by the other, and the abuser relinquishes his or her desire to be in control.[1]

In order for a power struggle to remain an integral part of any relationship, both people, regardless of their view of relationships, must engage in the same dynamic, which involves unspoken expectations and accumulated bitterness over unfulfilled demands.[2] Secrecy and silence are the two elements that keep power struggles alive, so this chapter is designed to help you unmask and give voice to those money-related issues that may be feeding the power differential in your relationship. We make the assumption that both of you view your relationship from the perspective of mutuality and that you agree that it is a major source of support for your personal growth and overall well-being.

SORTING IT OUT

In many ways money is the perfect focal point for power struggles in a relationship. As a culture, we equate having money with having power over other people. Many families teach by example that one person has control of the money and hence the power in the relationship. But the other person in this relationship will commonly figure out ways to try to regain some control. These techniques often fall into the passive-aggressive category. In other words, you may control how much money I get to spend on groceries, but I will balance the power scale. If you insist on punctuality, I will be chronically late. When you want sex, I'll have a headache. While my behavior is passive—I'm late or I have a headache—it is also aggressive because it is designed to get even in the face of your overt exercise of control over our money. Children watching this dynamic learn strong lessons about money, power, and being a victim.

As mentioned earlier, a power conflict between two people can be a way of each one attempting to have control over the other. This behavior can have varying foundations. Insecurity and low self-esteem often lead to attempts to control others. Unconsciously, this person believes "I don't feel good about myself and I want to hide that feeling, so I will try to make myself feel better by controlling everyone around me. I'll do that by putting them down. Then I'll feel up for a while." Fear of emotional intimacy also can underlie attempts to have power over others: "If I can control you, then I can keep you at a safe emotional distance, and I don't have to take the risk of revealing my feelings to you." Lacking the skills or the knowledge about how to relate in positive ways can keep an individual locked into believing one person in a relationship has to have the power and the other has to be the victim: "Partnering with someone who has a victim mentality enables me to have the unquestioned power in the relationship. This is comfortable for me and I don't have to explore other ways of relating." Most of us have encountered managers whose entire careers have been built on this one-up-one-down power structure. "My way or the highway" is their theme song. Unfortunately some organizations incorporate this philosophy into their corporate culture, an important point for business partners to consider.

Power struggles may also be the result of each person trying to hold onto old beliefs that just happen to contradict the partner's beliefs. We explored this situation when we discussed values in Chapter 7. As most of us know from experience, humans are quite adept at partnering with someone whose beliefs and characteristics are the opposite of ours. This tendency may be an unconscious attempt to balance our more extreme beliefs. It may also arise from the need to understand what the opposite behavior is like. If people who are committed to their own growth recognize this dynamic at play in their relationship, many options are open to them—as long as they are willing to abandon their opposing behaviors.

When we decide that we need to change a behavior, we naturally begin exploring other ways of behaving. Frequently we will go to the opposite extreme from the behavior we're trying to change simply because we have to know what that other behavior is like. Once we experience the opposing behavior, we now have a wide range of behaviors to choose from. If I've only explored the range from A to C, I don't have many choices. But once I've experienced A to Z, I have a lot of options and I am more apt to go with healthier, balanced behaviors. Experiencing the opposite behavior in our partner alleviates the necessity of experiencing it ourselves and shows us the range of possibilities falling between two extremes. Once we recognize this dynamic as a couple, we can begin moving away from trying to get the other to behave the way we do—the power struggle—and moving toward agreement and mutual support.

A DIFFERENT VIEW

All power struggles have the potential to end, stagnate, or stretch a relationship, especially those involving money. We're accustomed to the ending and stagnating possibilities these conflicts have, but what we want to explore is their ability to help your relationship grow and expand as all healthy, vibrant relationships do. For this kind of growth to occur, we need an uncommon perspective on power struggles coupled with the belief in mutuality as the defining principle of the relationship.

By their nature, power conflicts shine a light on parts of each person's hidden aspect, "the shadow," to use Jungian terminology. Each of us has a shadow containing many of our unpleasant characteristics that we do not want to look at or even admit to having. For example, females who were brought up to be "nice girls" will have difficulty admitting to being angry, even when anger is a perfectly normal and healthy response, as it is in an abusive situation, for instance. So the anger is pushed into the shadow where it festers, seeking some outlet. And it generally finds one—depression, outbursts of rage, or sniping at others with razor sarcasm are a few possibilities. The problem with the unacknowledged shadow is that unless the issues residing in it are recognized and, as much as possible, brought into the light and resolved, they will be projected onto the partner, often in sabotaging behaviors that damage the relationship and limit its growth. Because of our societal directive to stay secretive about money, our money-related beliefs and behaviors are often pushed into the shadow.

JANE AND DICK REVISITED

For example, suppose Jane grew up in a family where her father was the primary money earner who maintained control over how virtually all money was used. Her mother accepted this situation, happy to be taken care of financially. In spite of the fact that Jane was also brought up to earn her college degree and have a career, deep down she knew she had the right to be taken care of. When she married Dick, he looked like a good provider. Just as all of us do with our firmly held convictions, Jane accepted her belief in her right to be taken care of, so she never had a reason to discuss it with Dick and, in fact, may have denied that this tenet resided deep within her. After all, she could make her own way in the world. So this belief lives in Jane's shadow. Meanwhile, Dick was brought up to accept that he had to provide for his family, since that's what responsible male adults do. It's okay with him that Jane has a career since two incomes are needed these days to have all the nice things most people want.

So Jane and Dick look like a perfect match. If life were perfect, they might never have to deal with their unspoken beliefs. But what happens to them when some event illuminates their complementary yet unrealistic beliefs? How does Jane react if Dick is laid off and unable to find another job that pays him what he earned previously? How does Dick cope should his wife start earning more money than he does? What happens if Dick becomes incapacitated and cannot work? If the related money beliefs stay buried, Jane will probably resent Dick for no longer taking care of her financially and Dick will feel guilty for the same reason. These unacknowledged resentments will eventually affect how they treat each other. Often these secret angers are expressed as put-downs and seemingly minor insults, sarcasm, and cynicism. They tug and tear at the fabric of a relationship until it is in shreds, with both partners slouching off into their respective bitterness, neither fully understanding what happened to their perfect match.

Suppose, on the other hand, Jane and Dick had engaged in a full money discussion early on in their relationship. Or, when difficulties first started, they sat down together and worked their way through this book, discovering their unconscious but powerful expectations about what the other should and shouldn't do regarding money. In both scenarios, the dominant feeling is one of shared love and support for resolving the conflict and developing mutually healthy beliefs about generating money, thereby enhancing their individual growth and their relationship at the same time. If they take the approach that power struggles over money are an indication of what needs to be talked about and resolved so that the relationship can continue on a healthy path, Jane and Dick become a powerful unit for supporting each other through this transition. An added benefit of that approach is that their children learn a powerful, positive lesson by observing and experiencing how their parents handle adversity.

Business relationships are no different in the need for attention, honesty, and willingness to explore the money expectations each partner brings to every work day. As these individuals form a clearer understanding of each other's money issues and consciously decide to resolve conflicts as they arise, both the partnership and the business will flourish. Business partners have the same obligation as any other committed couple to break the silence of unspoken expectations they have for each other and to work toward a mutual harmonious belief system involving money

YEAH, BUT . . .

Even after discussing all these issues with a group at a workshop, someone usually insists that "Someone has to be in charge in a relationship." People who hold this belief see relationships as inherently out of balance, in so much constant conflict that one person must be the "grown-up" and maintain dominance. This rationalization can be used by an abuser to justify his or her desire to retain control. Or it can be used by the victim to maintain a familiar, if unhealthy, dynamic. It's this very imbalance that feeds power issues between two people and carries the possibility that one partner will be the abused and the other the abuser.

MUTUALITY AS THE FOUNDATION

What we are advocating here is developing a relationship based on shared power, with the primary focus on each person developing a sense of power over him- or herself. Achieving this state of self-power eliminates the desire to have power over other people, it guides an individual in voicing needs in a relationship, and gives that person the inner strength to look at his or her shadow with the intention of clearing away as many sabotaging issues as possible. An individual who is aligned with a sense of self-power refuses to take the power others may try to give away. Victims cannot stay victims when in a relationship with someone who stays attuned to his or her own self-power. That person will insist that the one playing the victim role stop giving away power and take responsibility for it on his or her own. In other words, a self-empowered individual stops participating in the power struggle, thus forcing her or his partner to do the same.

Your family genogram, your exploration of your attitudes, emotions, and values concerning money gives you a head start in achieving this goal. As you take ownership of the beliefs and issues you bring to your relationship, dragging some of them out of your shadow, you become clearer about embracing your chosen money beliefs and building the kind of relationship you want with money. You stop giving your power to negative money beliefs and are less likely to be emotionally jerked around when some near and dear belief is threatened. This situation enables you to engage in productive discussions about money issues with your partner, working to develop mutually shared power. You have grown as an individual, and your relationship has improved as well. Two self-empowered people work together in pursuit of creative problem solving rather than exhausting their energy in power struggles just to prove themselves right and the other wrong.

In this dynamic relationship, who makes how much money is irrelevant. Responsibilities related to paying bills, maintaining a budget, saving for special purchases, and for retirement are all shared. It matters less who does what and more that both are making what each feels is an equal contribution. The rewards include more financial stability in the relationship, less stress, a diffusing of significant power issues, and a subsequent increase in energy for fun activities.

Power struggles are the major stumbling block to the natural evolution of any relationship into something greater than the sum of its parts. Once the money-related struggles are under control, the mechanism used to deal with them can be applied to other power struggles as well. Power-related distractions and interferences fall away from the relationship's vital dynamic. Eventually, the energy that was tied up in the conflicts is freed, allowing the couple to experience a new, stable foundation. This base becomes the fertile ground for planting and nurturing new beliefs (Chapter 12) and for cultivating the beauty of a healthy relationship. As we frequently remind clients, the most lush gardens have a lot of compost in the soil!

TIES BETWEEN POWER AND MONEY

Let's start our exploration by asking what associations you have with power and money. We suggest that you each examine these questions, writing down your responses before talking them over with each other.

How are money and power connected?

On a scale of 1 to 9, with 9 being the most powerful, where do you place yourself when you think about your financial situation?

Who is more powerful when it comes to money, you or your partner? What are the reasons for this? Do you think your partner would agree with your answer? Why or why not?

Have you ever used money as a weapon against your partner? How? Has your partner ever used money as a weapon against you? How?

Who makes more money in your relationship? How do you feel about that?

By looking at your responses to these questions, you can begin to understand how you relate power and money, and the role this correlation plays in your relationship with another person.

ALICE'S STORY

Alice, a woman who attended one of our workshops, told us about a time when she was out of work and her partner offered to cover food and utility bills until she got another job. This financial support meant that she could take more time looking for a job she really wanted, rather than taking something out of desperation. Alice said that she and her partner discussed this proposal at length because of her concern about the inequity. She has always been self-supporting. Her partner insisted that she wanted to extend this temporary support out of love, so Alice agreed. She kept contributing her part of the mortgage payments, but all other household expenses were covered by her partner. This arrangement lasted about six months until Alice was once again fully employed in a job she wanted. Unfortunately, Alice learned that the offer was not as freely given as she had understood.

While Alice was out of work, her partner began scrutinizing her purchases, reminding her that if she couldn't pay her share of the household expenses, she couldn't buy herself anything but necessities. And new clothes, she was told, were not in that category. Even after Alice found a job, her partner suggested maintaining the financial situation until she "got back on her feet." But since Alice had already noticed a shift in the power structure of their relationship, she insisted upon paying her share of all expenses as she had previously. For almost a year after the full financial support stopped, her partner would remind Alice that she had "supported" her, using a tone that Alice interpreted as meaning "I'm the one with the money, so I'm in charge."

Meanwhile, the additional housework Alice had done during the time she was unemployed—her attempt to "balance the accounts"—went unacknowledged. Alice's assumption was that her partner would notice and honor her additional contributions, but she never mentioned this. So both women kept their silence and secrecy about this changed money and power dynamic. Alice finally asked her partner to stop bringing up the long-gone financial imbalance and attempted to have a discussion about what she considered her partner's power and control issues. Her partner denied any such motivation and stopped bringing up her "sacrifice," as she described it.

While the two continued to share expenses equally for the rest of their time together, Alice told us that she never really trusted her partner as much as she had prior to the incident. She had experienced her partner's covert attempts to assert control over her with the promise of unfettered financial support followed by overt behaviors intended to control Alice's money-related behaviors. She felt she had been told one motivation was behind the offer only to discover a very different one. The financial imbalance was accompanied by her partner's increasingly obvious attempts to exert control over Alice and her spending. Alice did admit that she never pushed her partner to have a thorough discussion about what happened. So money attitudes in this relationship went underground, with neither partner willing to share financial accounts or create joint savings for such cooperative activities as vacations or retirement. They had no mutual financial goals. Each was on her own and eventually this contributed to their break-up.

This dynamic between Alice and her partner also illustrates what can happen when two people with differing views of relationships get together. Alice believed in mutuality and assumed that her partner did as well. The partner, on the other hand, behaved like someone who believed that relationships always involve one person in control and the other being controlled. In this case, money was the means for bringing out this difference, although many years passed before Alice fully realized what had happened and was able to tell us her story.

GETTING TO THE ROOTS

Looking again at your family genogram, see if you can pinpoint the roots of some of your beliefs about money and power. We suggest you write down your responses to the following questions as you examine your family and other messages concerning money and power. This act helps clarify your thoughts and discharge associated emotions, making a discussion with your partner about these issues easier. It also helps to break the cycle of silence and secrecy that fuels power struggles.

What power struggles did you experience in your family? Who had the power in your parents' relationship?

What connections were made between money and power and the use of that power in your family? Did someone play the passive-aggressive role in the power dynamic? In other words, did one person control the money while the other one withheld affection, insulted the other, or made other similar attempts to balance the power?

What did you learn from siblings or other relatives about money and power?

What did you learn from your family about business, power, and money?

Which of these messages do you now hold and how do you play them out in your relationship?

Now let's examine your cultural, societal, and religious messages for the same types of beliefs. Referring back to Chapter 4 might be helpful at this point. There are many aspects of culture and religion to look at, including spoken and unspoken beliefs arising from music, advertising, news, television shows, sports, and so on. Try to focus on those areas in which you received the most powerful messages. For someone brought up with unlimited TV-viewing privileges, the influence of this medium will be very different than it is for someone who grew up watching little television.

During this exploration, pay attention to whether or not your family messages reinforced or contradicted the cultural messages you absorbed. Carrying opposing messages about money is quite common. It's one of the things that can make your behavior inconsistent. It may be the reason your partner may look like a penny-pincher in one situation and a spendthrift in another. These contradictions can arise from within the family—Mom gives us one belief while Dad gives us the opposite—or they can come from the clash of our family messages meeting our cultural beliefs. As you look at the money beliefs you derived from your culture, society, and religion, pay special attention to any that are contrary to your family messages and be aware of how you resolved this conflict.

What societal notions about money have I adopted? Think about ideas such as "My worth as a person is determined by how much money I make" or "He who has the most toys, wins."

How do these beliefs keep power and money in relationship with each other?

What beliefs do you hold around money and power in the workplace?

What cultural messages influence you when you make major purchases?

How would you summarize this culture's predominant beliefs in regard to power and money? What is your response to those beliefs?

Before you begin discussing your responses to these questions with your partner, we would like you to consider two more questions.

If you identify and let go of your beliefs about power and money, how will this change your behavior?

How will it change your relationship with your partner?

Sometimes we cling to old beliefs because we're not sure what it would mean to us in terms of our behavior to let them go. Having in mind a healthy alternative to our outmoded beliefs and behaviors assists us in making a change. And it helps us to be more open when talking about these messages with our partner, since we are no longer so emotionally tied to the old way of thinking and reacting.

HAVING A SUCCESSFUL DISCUSSION

In the course of discussing these emotionally charged issues with your partner, we suggest that you both agree to several points at the outset. First, agree to choose a time when you will both feel up to the discussion, so that neither is stressed or exhausted. Conversely, avoid using time when you may normally be engaged in some recreational activity. For example, if you traditionally go out for an unwinding-from-the-week dinner on Friday evenings, don't bring up money issues during the meal. Next, stipulate that neither of you will be interrupted while discussing your beliefs. The phone gets turned off, the children are asleep or out of the house, pagers and cell phones are off. Also agree on the amount of time you wish to devote to the discussion, realizing that you probably won't cover all issues in one sitting. It's more important to thoroughly air out one topic feeding a power struggle than to cover several issues superficially.

Finally, plan to stop your talk if either of you becomes defensive. Rising anger or fear are definite signals that this is happening. Actually, they are excellent clues to deep-seated issues that may be troubling to you and the relationship, concerns that need to be brought out into the open. If defensiveness arises, it's appropriate to voice that feeling and take a break. The person who is getting upset might say something like, "I'm starting to feel angry about this discussion. I need to take some deep breaths." Both of you must agree to honor this need for a break by stopping the discussion and resuming it when the time is right. This isn't an excuse to once again bury the sensitive issue. If it isn't dealt with, it will come up again, often in a nasty way, a phenomenon all of us have experienced. When you both agree to take a break, set another time for revisiting the topic.

All these suggestions also apply to business partners as they work through their money conflicts. Monday morning is probably not a good time to have this kind of discussion because too many business-related activities are taking place. Friday afternoon may not be the best time either, since you both may be tired from the week and anxious to begin a relaxing weekend. Furthermore, if anything goes unresolved—and we hope that would not happen— one of you will be carrying that feeling for several days over the weekend, which is not good. So choose a time that is the best for both of you, knowing that you are taking an important step toward ensuring your success.

Sometimes a neutral third party is needed to facilitate such discussions, but often couples can manage these talks themselves as long as they stay focused on the love, or the business plan, that brought them together in the first place. At the end of each session, do a quick review to remind yourselves what you have accomplished and to reinforce what you have done. In other words, build in your own positive reinforcement. This summary also gives each of you the opportunity to make sure you have both heard the same things.

IT TAKES TIME

Resolving these power issues will undoubtedly take several discussions. Give this process time. We would all like our deepest problems to be cleared and gone in a half-hour, with time out for commercials, but true resolution comes much more slowly. We also have to be willing to tolerate some discomfort along the way. Sometimes a discussion that is focused on one issue brings up other problems we weren't aware of. We have to be willing to be uncomfortable and to resist the quick fix or an attempt to dismiss the issue, either of which may make us feel better in the short run but will worsen things in the long run. Remember, you and your partner are working to give a voice to those messages that drive people either to try to control another person by controlling money, or to abdicate their power over themselves and their money by giving it to their partner. Eventually the power struggle will hit the fan, resulting in severe damage to the relationship.

The goal in identifying and diffusing power/money issues is to participate in a partnership where power is shared so that the relationship continues to evolve into a stable source of energy and love for all involved.

MOVING FORWARD ▶▶▶▶▶▶▶▶

Our intention in this chapter is to encourage open discussions about power and money to help couples eliminate struggles over control and embrace mutuality. The following actions help accomplish this goal:

1. Explore your associations between power and money by writing down your answers to the questions under "Ties Between Power and Money."

2. Discuss your responses with your partner.

3. Examine your genogram for the sources of your beliefs about money and power. Use the questions under "Getting to the Roots" as a guide.

4. Look for sources of these messages outside your family, referring to the second set of questions under "Getting to the Roots."

5. Discuss what you've learned with your partner, following the suggestions for successful discussions.

6. Give yourselves time for multiple discussions to work out the issues that arise.

10

LOVE, SEX, AND MONEY

"**M**oney can't buy me love," says an old Beatles' song. Well, maybe not. Some people however, would say that money can buy a lot, including companionship, forgiveness, and even sex. We see examples of this in our everyday lives, as well as in the films and television shows we watch. In this chapter, we look at the money/sex connection. We discuss how money and sex relate and how the combination can be misused. And we'll offer some suggestions on how to keep the connections clear and healthy.

Keep in mind as we discuss this topic that it can be highly complex. Sex and money are two of the most difficult subjects to talk about in our culture. On its own, each is fraught with secrecy and shame. And each has the potential to trigger a variety of complex feelings ranging from self-doubt all the way to anger. When we put money and sex together, they intensify each other's effect and become highly charged with many conflicting and powerful emotions. These emotions make this topic a challenging one.

You will probably also notice considerable overlap of topics covered here and in other chapters. Again, the complexity of sex and money means that these issues do not fall within clear-cut boundaries. Whether we are talking about Cultural Messages (Chapter 4), Money and Self-Worth (Chapter 5), Money and Secrecy (Chapter 8), or The Power Differential (Chapter 9), sex enters the picture. And because sexual dysfunction in a relationship frequently is a symptom of some other problem, you may find sex to be a focal point for still other issues. Money is one of the mediums we can use to play out sexual issues. This being so, when issues connected with money and sex come together, they can become so convoluted and complex that it is difficult to sort it all out. Let's begin by looking at a familiar sex and money connection.

PAYING FOR COMPANIONSHIP

Recently, National Public Radio featured a series of interviews with centenarians. One poignant story concerned a 104-year-old former cowboy and preacher, Roy Larkin Stamper. He had settled in the Oklahoma territory as a boy and grew up on the frontier. As he discussed his current life situation, Mr. Stamper said that his biggest need was for a companion. Acknowledging the likelihood that "one I'd have probably wouldn't have me," he went on to say that he had a lot he could offer a woman: income, property, and a car. A follow-up story one year later reported Stamper's death at 105.[1] We learned that he did indeed find a companion as a result of the radio story. Whether the trade-off worked out for both parties, we can only speculate. We certainly hope so. But it is clear that in this case, money could buy the companionship he sought.

Other more public figures have found themselves seeking love and companionship in similar ways. Doris Duke, heiress to the vast American Tobacco Company fortunes, was a prime example. As a child, Doris seemed to have it all. Once, for instance, her father hired an entire circus to entertain Doris and two of her cousins at their country estate. Her father's wealth gave her luxuries and exotic experiences other children only fantasize about. Doris grew up with everything except self-confidence. Her father reportedly told her, "You are too tall, too rich, and too unattractive for any man to ever love you for yourself."[2] Apparently she believed him, because she spent her life in relationships with men who treated her badly and were after her money. In the last years of her life, her butler somehow gained control of her money and, according to some reports, may even have contributed to her death. Although she left the world a legacy of philanthropic works and good deeds, Duke's personal life was problematic, and her search for love and companionship was a miserable failure.

Another instance of the apparent exchange of money for companionship and youth shocked even the usually unflappable Hollywood. When aspiring actress Anna Nicole Smith married the wealthy J.

Howard Marshall II, the 63-year difference in their ages raised many an eyebrow. In spite her protestation that, "I don't care what people think. I love him, and we're in love and that's it," the gossip columnists speculated that he was attempting to buy a companion while she was looking for wealth.[3] The battle over Marshall's estate after his death brought further conflict between Smith and Marshall's son—and a lawsuit. Whether this was truly a love match is open for debate. In a culture that fosters the belief that the only way the wealthy can get love is to buy it, matches such as this one do give the appearance of buying companionship.

Hugh Hefner, of Playboy Enterprise fame, is another example of someone who seemingly pays for female companionship. When he turned 70, Hefner was interviewed by Terry Gross of Boston Public Radio's *Fresh Air*. At the time Hefner was living with three young women, all under the age of 20. When questioned about the potential rewards of the living arrangement, he claimed they all enjoyed each other's company, and the fun they had together was the basis for their relationship. His wealth and fame had nothing to do with it, according to Hefner.[4] Maybe he was reading the situation correctly. One has to wonder, however, if the young women would find Mr. Hefner's company as enjoyable if he were a retired autoworker living on a pension. Somehow we doubt it.

There are plenty of other, less exalted, instances of money's ability to buy attractive companionship. An owner of a cab company told us about a regular customer who can no longer drive herself around town and so depends on cabs for all her transportation needs. This elderly woman is willing to pay a premium price to have the company's most attractive cab driver at her disposal. There is nothing sexual in the arrangement. The woman just likes to be driven around town by a handsome man. And since she can pay for it, this is exactly what happens.

CONFUSING LOVE AND MATERIAL GOODS

A successful professional woman told of this experience with a lover.

"We started out having a really good relationship. He was witty, dynamic, and fun to be with. He also was unemployed for most of the time we were together. His expectation was that because I had the better job, I should pay for entertainment and other items that he couldn't. Things came to a head when he wanted me to buy him a truck. I refused, and after that the relationship just deteriorated. We eventually broke up. Looking back on it now, I am not sure if he really cared about me or was just into what I could buy for him. I learned a valuable lesson from that relationship."

The woman's experience is not unique. We have heard of other relationships in which a similar dynamic was present. The relationship was based more on material things than on genuine love and commitment. And when the material things went, so did the relationship. Sadly, when this happens, the person who has money learns to be distrustful of any relationship. "How do I know whether someone is with me because of who I am or because of what I have?" asked one woman plaintively. "It is really difficult to trust anyone."

Are we saying that it is impossible to have a loving relationship if you have money? Certainly not. We are saying that money can complicate a relationship in many ways, especially when people don't take the time to get their priorities straight.

STAYING TOGETHER FOR ALL THE WRONG REASONS

We all know couples who stay together long after the love has gone. They just don't want to face being alone. This is a sad situation because it is so empty and unfulfilling. Neither person is happy, yet neither will take any steps to change the situation. The status quo is not ideal, but the partners seem to agree that it is better that living alone. "We don't have a lot in common anymore, but I am too old to start over," said Tom, a 60-year-old man discussing his 40-year marriage to Marge. "Besides, I don't want to be alone." This type of arrangement also allows both people to avoid the emotional risks tied to true intimacy.

Sometimes parents will provide support to their adult children in return for their company. Again, the fear of being alone outweighs the inconvenience of supporting a grown child. "I am happy that he is still living with me," one woman told us, speaking of her 40-

year-old son. "I support him for the most part. He makes his own spending money and I pay for the rest. It has its drawbacks, but since I have always been afraid of living alone, it works for me."

The story of money buying companionship is an old one. We see the wealth/companionship link frequently portrayed in the movies. But it looks more glamorous on screen than in real life. In *Pretty Woman,* a wealthy businessman pays a hooker to be his companion for a series of social events. Money can buy companionship in this case, along with luxury hotels, visits to the opera, fancy meals, and a fantastic wardrobe. Plus, what starts out as paid companionship (naturally) turns into true love. This is Hollywood, after all. In most other cases, paid companionship remains just that, with all of the complications and potential for hurt.

Probably as long as there are lonely people in the world, there will be attempts to buy love and companionship. There is really nothing inherently wrong with this arrangement if it works out for all concerned. But frequently it does not. Parents get tired of supporting grown children and become angry and resentful. Jilted lovers, ex-spouses, and former live-in companions regularly engage in vicious legal battles when they believe they have been cheated out of what is rightfully theirs. The intensity of these struggles, along with the anger they generate, make us wonder how loving the relationship was to begin with.

PAYING TO BE FREE OF A RELATIONSHIP

The flip side of paying for companionship is paying to be free of a person once the relationship is no longer working. Johnny Carson once jokingly said that Hollywood divorces are expensive "Because they are worth it."[5] Celebrity-watchers can list numerous instances of expensive and acrimonious divorces. The tabloids are full of such tales, and each week brings a new illustration of just what people will spend to rid themselves of someone they no longer love. For example, Joan Collins paid $1,000,000 to be free of record executive Ron Kass. Jane Fonda shed Tom Hayden for $10 million. Joan Lunden paid $18,000 monthly alimony to ex-husband Michael Krauss.[6] The list goes on and on. It has been said that the one who wants out of a marriage is the one who pays the most.[7] This seems to be true for divorces of the rich and famous, as well as the not-so-famous.

Even brilliant people find themselves buying their way out of a love that has cooled. Albert Einstein reportedly gave the proceeds of his Nobel Prize to his first wife, Mileva, because he wanted a divorce so he could marry another woman. Marry her he did. His first wife used the money to buy investment real estate. Hopefully both parties found it a fair bargain.[8]

Couples who are not famous face the same issues on a less grand scale. The partner who wants out is likely to be willing to pay off the reluctant partner. An educator we know told of giving his first wife the house, car, and the rights to his retirement pension because he wanted to be free to marry another woman he had fallen in love with. "It left me financially strapped," he said, "but it was worth it to be able to be with her."

Sometimes, the reverse happens—people feel they can't afford to break up with a partner. A woman may remain in an abusive relationship, for example, because she lacks the money for attorney fees and living costs. Or couples may stay together because it is too costly to separate; they convince themselves that splitting assets is just too expensive or difficult, so the relationship continues. In 1990 an article titled "Live-in Divorce: Tortured Couples Who Have to Stay Together," appeared in *New York Magazine.*[9] The story detailed the lives of couples who couldn't afford to split up and so lived together but maintained separate lives. They weren't necessarily happy, but the arrangement fit their financial needs.

Another couple we know was no longer in love, and indeed, could barely tolerate each other. Yet they stayed together because they both owned a number of shares in the family business. A divorce would cause a major shift in the balance of power in the corporation, and neither wanted that to happen.

Money, in these cases, is given the power in the relationship. Both people abdicate their self-power, assigning it to money. Neither individual has to take responsibility for being in a dysfunctional partnership. The inanimate financial assets become the most powerful aspect of the relationship. And this power determines whether or how they split up. An unwanted spouse or companion can be bought off. Freedom is available for a price. Just as we can buy love, we can use money to be free of unwanted love. Or we use it to decide that staying connected is the better option. Either way, money is allowed to be the determining factor.

BUYING FORGIVENESS

"Exactly How Mad Is She?" reads the sign on a flower-delivery van. This slogan, surrounded by bouquets of roses, is a reminder that it is an accepted practice to secure forgiveness by buying flowers. Or candy. Or better still, diamonds. This is an old idea. Men are supposed to buy women's forgiveness with gifts. And there is some evidence that it works. A recent study sponsored by Enesco Corporation questioned 1,100 individuals about gift giving habits and feelings. Seventy-three percent of the women surveyed disclosed that they feel special and loved when they receive gifts, as compared to 56 percent of the men. Women are also more likely than men to express gratitude with a hug or kiss for gifts received.[10] If a conflict has occurred, it seems that gift giving *is* a way of obtaining forgiveness.

Money can buy forgiveness, and sex is frequently part of the bargain. In a recent *Redbook Magazine* survey, 72 percent of the women responding revealed that they withhold sex from their husbands when they fight.[11] If withholding sex can be a way of dealing with conflict, it would follow that giving gifts would be a way to break through the conflict. So in effect, gifts can buy forgiveness and thus sex. Joan Rivers said: "God gave women sex so we can shop the next day."[12] Clearly she understood the money, forgiveness, and sex connection.

The idea of buying forgiveness in relationships is a common one. One woman told us that when she is angry with her husband, she goes shopping and charges items to his account. "I figure he owes me," she said. "If he can spend all that time with his golf buddies, then he can pay my clothes-shopping bill. If I shop while he is still feeling guilty about being gone, he just pays the bill without saying anything. It is kind of an unspoken agreement we have that if he wants forgiveness, I get to shop."

THE MONEY/SEX CONNECTION

"Goodness, what beautiful diamonds," gushed a friend, eyeing Mae West's stunning necklace. Mae, in her inimitable manner, reportedly replied, "Goodness had nothing to do with it."[13]

In her book *Kept Women*, author Leslie McRay recounts the experiences of a number of women who lived a life of luxury and excitement by allowing themselves to be "kept" by wealthy men. In such an arrangement, according to McRay, the woman is provided with a living situation that includes fine dining, expensive clothes, luxury cars, and fancy apartments. What is expected in return is that the she be available for an exclusive sexual relationship at times specified by the man. The lifestyle has appeal, according to the author, because "Most of us like the idea of being viewed as an object of worship, respect, and adoration by the opposite sex. We like the idea of being pampered and desired by the rich, powerful, and famous."[14] The appeal of a life of luxury is what leads women to allow themselves to be kept; the seduction of the lifestyle is what keeps them there.

In most instances the exchange of money or gifts for sexual favors takes a more subtle form. A woman is taken out for a lavish night on the town. A husband may bring his wife flowers and candy. A woman may buy supplies for and prepare an elaborate meal and serve it by candlelight. The usual expectation is that sex will follow a romantic evening. This is a case of money and sex being linked in a harmless way. Both parties get what they want out of an arrangement that they both agree to, and nobody gets hurt.

In other instances, however, such is not the case. There are times when the money and sex link can be hurtful. A recent ABC program looking into sexual attitudes and rape interviewed some men who believed that if a man spent money on a woman, he was entitled to sex at the end of the evening.[15] The idea of "owed" sex is incredibly dangerous and demeaning to all involved. This is an instance in which the linking of money and sex is clearly inappropriate.

In the 1993 film *Indecent Proposal*, a happily married young couple goes to Las Vegas in the hopes of winning some money to get out of a financial bind. The young woman catches the eye of a handsome millionaire. He offers the couple a million dollars if the wife will spend one night with him. What this offer does to the couple's relationship and how their feelings toward themselves and each other change shape the plot of this film. The young husband and wife struggle with their own money issues as they try to decide how to handle the situation. The millionaire's offer is repugnant yet attractive—a classic moral dilemma. The film becomes a metaphor for the damage a misplaced focus on sex and money can bring to a relationship.

In ordinary life, most of us get no such offer and thus never need to struggle with our scruples. We do experience that money and sex connection on a smaller scale however. One woman explained that sex was part of a Friday payday routine she and her husband shared. "He stops off at the bar on his way home after getting paid. He spends time with his drinking buddies and some of his check goes for that. Then the next day I go shopping for groceries for the coming week. Then, on Saturday night, we have really great sex. It may not make sense to anyone else, but it works for us. There is just something about that money that is a turn-on for us."

Money can also have the opposite effect. Marta told us this story: "Toward the end of my marriage, I started making more money than Jason. I noticed our sex life gradually deteriorated to practically nothing. The more money I made, the worse our sex life got. Was there a connection? I truly believe that my increase in income was the final straw for us."

MONEY, SEX, AND BUSINESS

Sex and business are frequently joined. Sometimes this link brings negative results, sometimes the results are positive. Rarely are they neutral. As we have seen so far, combining sex and money gives us one highly volatile compound. Placing this volatility into the world of business increases its power exponentially. Let's look at some of the issues and problems that can result when we mix sex, money, and business.

One of the most notorious combinations of the three elements is the stereotype of the casting room couch. The idea that aspiring stars, usually women but not always, were expected to provide sexual favors in return for a film role is accepted Hollywood lore. And it seems to have some basis in fact. As Marilyn Monroe said, "You can't sleep your way into being a star. It takes much, much more—but it helps."[16] Comedienne Phyllis Diller stated, "The casting couch is the name of the game in Hollywood. I know there are stars, especially women, who have made a career from sexual favors."[17] In recent years, the enactment of legislation prohibiting sexual harassment has called a halt to some of the more blatant abuses of the sex/money/business connection. But in some industries, the practice continues. It has simply gone underground.

Frequently we see relationships between a young woman and an older, more powerful, man. It has been said that power is the greatest aphrodisiac. An alliance with an older mentor may help the young woman's career, or it may hold her up for humiliation and ridicule. Did Monica Lewinsky profit from her association with a powerful man? Only she can accurately answer this question. Certainly it opened some career doors that would otherwise have been closed to her. It also held her up to public scrutiny of a type that no young woman should have to endure. Her story is not atypical. As we discussed in the earlier chapter on the Power Differential (Chapter 9), an imbalance of power always leads to some kind of attempt to equalize the situation. And it holds the potential for huge amounts of hurt.

The sleep-your-way-to-success stereotype is also perpetuated in the business world. Many a successful woman has been accused of "sleeping her way to the top," a charge seldom leveled at a man. This accusation is hurtful because it negates the hard work and effort that it took for the woman to attain success in her career.

That's not to say that work and sex (and love) should never mix. The reality is that many people do form love relationships at work. It just makes sense to find yourself attracted to someone with whom you spend most of your waking hours. In addition to spending large amounts of time with a co-worker, you also have the opportunity to see him or her in good times and bad, fair moods and foul. You learn how that person handles stress and pressure. You see caring and heartless aspects. Developing a love relationship is understandable under the circumstances. But just because it is understandable doesn't mean it is trouble-free. As co-workers whose relationships have gone bad can attest, some of the most troublesome work-related problems come from break-ups of a love relationship. And if the former lovers had a superior-inferior work relationship, a break-up can cause careers to be stalled, raises withheld, or even jobs lost.

We know of cases where business partners have fallen in love and ruined a formerly workable business relationship. Again, inserting sex and money into the business mix has the potential to cause problems. One couple we know had a successful landscaping business. As they worked together, their attraction to each other grew. They ended up leaving their respective spouses to be together. After their marriage they found themselves swamped with the pressures of running a business and building a life together. They had to balance the demands of a new marriage with the needs in their children's lives as they tried to blend their formerly separate families into one. Differing child-rearing styles as well as totally dissimilar spending habits surfaced. The couple found themselves arguing constantly. Eventually, the marriage broke up. The resulting animosity was enough to finish off the formerly prosperous business as well. One partner/spouse bought the other out and struggled along for a short period of time. Eventually the business folded.

This is not to say that a marriage of co-workers is always doomed to failure. Or that a personal relationship with a business partner will consistently result in a disaster for the couple and the business. We are aware of business partnerships that have withstood the challenge of becoming an intimate relationship. The relationships that succeed, however, are composed of people who have a firm grip on all aspects of their money issues. They understand their personal and business money-related behaviors and messages and have a history of open discussions about money. With this foundation, they can then form intimate relationships without letting sex and money cloud their judgment. The money/sex/business connection is an area that requires clarity about one's money issues. Without this clear vision, the results can be disastrous.

BREAKING THE MONEY/SEX CONNECTION

As you work your way through this book, you are no doubt beginning to see some of the ways you can approach money in a healthier manner. Breaking the money/sex connection is one of the most important ways you can have a healthier relationship with your partner and with money. Whether you are looking at your relationship with an intimate partner or a business partner, achieving clarity in your money issues will pay huge dividends.

The following are some suggestions for working through the issues.

Suggestion One—Become Aware of Old Patterns

This would be an ideal time to go back to your genogram to check for any of the patterns we have discussed. As we have emphasized, we are not automatically doomed to repeat old family patterns. Knowing about the existence of patterns gives us the power to consciously make new choices.

Do you see any money/sex connections within your genogram? List and briefly describe them below.

Which of these patterns are active in your relationship? List and briefly describe them below.

Here is what one of our workshop participants discovered:

As she studied her genogram, Nancy began to see a strong pattern of buying forgiveness. It was especially evident in her parents' relationship. "I can remember the heavy air of tension in the house when my Mother and Dad fought. It was almost like a play, and they both knew their roles so well. After a fight, Mother would become cold, silent, and unforgiving. Dad would pretend her anger didn't bother him, but even as a kid, I could tell he got really nervous when she withdrew like that. So he would bring gifts to her to try and win her over. She would hold out until he hit upon just the right gift, and then her coldness would begin to melt. After a while, their relationship would return to normal until the next fight/make-up cycle began again. I just hated watching that, so I was absolutely appalled to realize that I was doing a similar thing with Brad. It wasn't as blatant as with my parents, but I realized that I do have a withdrawal pattern. When Brad brings me flowers after a fight, it usually signals that we are ready to forget our anger and get on with our lives."

Suggestion Two—Break Old Patterns

After identifying the money/sex connections, you can make a new plan. What is the appropriate place for money in your relationship? How can you make money serve you and your partner in a more appropriate way?

Again, let's look at Nancy's story for an example of making changes. After identifying her pattern of expecting Brad to "buy" her forgiveness, Nancy was ready to make a new plan. She and Brad had a discussion about how their behavior patterns kept them both stuck in the old way of relating, with Nancy withdrawing and Brad cajoling her back into a better mood. They decided they wanted to try something different. They set up some ground rules for their disagreements and began to hold family discussions. They made a commitment that they both would continue these discussions until there was a resolution of the issue at hand.

Nancy and Brad found that by following their ground rules and using good communication techniques, they were able to handle most issues without resorting to their old pattern. Each time they were able to come to a mutually agreeable solution, they chose some couple's activity as a reward. They might go out to dinner, take in a movie, or visit a new exhibit at their local museum. Instead of Brad taking the responsibility for buying Nancy's forgiveness, the couple found a way to reward themselves for a new behavior pattern. And the couple's activities served to strengthen their relationship bond. So they received a double benefit—a stronger relationship and a method of working out conflicts.

Suggestion Three—Start Living the New Patterns

Changing our behavior is a challenge. But when we meet our challenges and succeed in making healthy changes, we are rewarded for our efforts by the good feelings that result. We can begin to catch ourselves when we slip into the old, unsatisfactory behavior patterns. Once we catch ourselves, we can substitute new behaviors for the old ones. Soon the new behaviors replace the old habits and the change becomes permanent.

Suggestion Four—Know When to Seek Help

This book is designed to help you understand and change old behavior patterns. For that reason, you will find case studies, exercises, and suggestions throughout this book. Sometimes, however, couples need more than a book to help them solve their problems. Both Diane and Kay have been in long-term relationships and recognize that sometimes couples need the assistance of a cool-headed third party. If you find yourselves at an impasse that looks insurmountable, get outside help. You can find counselors and therapists listed in your local phone directory. Or you may choose to utilize the services of a spiritual advisor or counselor. If you have come this far in the book, it's evident that you already see your relationship as worth the effort it takes to preserve it. Sometimes seeking outside help is an excellent way of making that effort a success.

MOVING FORWARD ▶▶▶▶▶▶▶▶▶

This chapter discussed some of the unhealthy ways love, sex, and money can be connected in a relationship. Breaking the money/sex connection is one of the most important ways you can have a healthier relationship with your partner and with money. Whether you are looking at your relationship with an intimate partner or a business partner, achieving clarity in your money issues will pay huge dividends. Here are some steps you can take to make sure that love, sex, and money are not linked in unhealthy ways in your relationship.

1. List any of the money/sex connections that you have become aware of as you read this chapter. Put an asterisk by those you believe are most damaging to your relationship. Select one of these as your first target.

2. List any changes you would like to make in your relationship with your partner. Prioritize them, placing the most important items at the top of your list.

3. Develop an action plan listing the changes you wish to make. Commit yourself to the changes you would like to make by writing them in your journal or another appropriate place.

4. Share your action plan with your partner. How can you and your partner work together to achieve your plan?

PART 3

Making Plans: Developing a Couples Vision of Money

11

COUPLES COMMUNICATION

One of the most important steps you and your partner can take to keep your money relationship on the right track is learning and using effective communication skills. Sounds easy, right? We communicate all the time, don't we? Well, not exactly. In fact, difficulty in communicating is one of the top reasons why couples end up in therapists' offices. Because of the emotion involved, adding money to the mix almost guarantees problems. That's the bad news. The good news is that effective communication skills can be learned. And when they are, you will notice a dramatic difference in your life. You will feel better about yourself, your partner, and your relationship. Misunderstandings will be minimized; trust will be maximized. You will be well on your way to more positive and productive interactions. This process will take effort on the part of both of you. But since you have come this far in this book, we assume you are committed to making changes.

Do we believe that men and women are so different in their communication styles that they seem to be from different planets? Or that same-sex couples have the edge in communication because they don't have gender differences to contend with? No. Do we believe that all couples struggle with communication at times? Absolutely, yes! But communication doesn't have to be such a struggle. You can take some of the conflict out of your interactions by applying some of the suggestions we'll provide in this chapter.

Throughout this book we have designed activities to help you communicate more effectively. In this chapter we present some practical strategies you can use to strengthen your communication skills. We focus on developing skills to use when discussing your money issues, but you will be able to apply the general principles to other areas as well. You will see improvement as you put these strategies into practice. We will also discuss some options for further growth, including some of the more popular couples communication training programs. If you wish to take a class or workshop to improve your skills, these suggestions will give you a place to start looking.

RAISING YOUR COMMUNICATION IQ (INTERACTION QUOTIENT): A TWO-STEP PLAN

Your communication interaction quotient is the ability to communicate clearly and effectively with another person. This ability consists of equal parts of speaking and listening. Raising your communication IQ takes time and effort. The payoff is an improved relationship. Couples who communicate well can decrease their conflict, increase their closeness, and generally feel better about themselves and their partner. In your efforts to improve your relationship with each other and with money, you will find that raising your communication IQ is one of the most helpful efforts you can make. The results will be well worth the effort expended.

Step One: Develop Your Listening Skills

Listening is one of those skills we tend to take for granted. Barring a physical disability, we have been *hearing* since we first came into the world. So we assume we are doing it effectively. Usually we aren't. We tend to forget that there is a huge difference between hearing and listening. Hearing is a passive process while listening takes active effort. Improving your listening ability gives you a major advantage in any relationship. With some effort, you will find yourself really listening instead of merely hearing.

We All Have Bad Habits Listening is hard. There is no doubt about it. For most of us, speaking comes more easily than listening. And we all have some bad habits when it comes to listening. Have you ever:

Found yourself refocusing on a conversation with your partner, only to realize that your mind drifted and you missed at least the last third of what was said?

Used the time your partner was talking to formulate your own response, so that you heard very little of your partner's actual words?

Mentally composed a "to do" list instead of giving your full attention to what was being said?

Decided that you really didn't need to listen to what your partner was saying, because you had heard it all a dozen times before?

Interrupted your partner in the middle of a sentence to insert your own point of view?

Become so angry with your partner that you just couldn't bear to listen anymore?

Started judging what your partner was saying and gotten so distracted that you missed the main points she/he was trying to make?

You have probably done all of the above at some point in your relationship. We all have. We don't mean to be rude or uncaring, we just have acquired some bad listening habits along the way. It's no wonder. Most of us have never been taught to listen. So until we get into a relationship where our listening habits become an issue, we don't even realize that we lack the skills.

The reality is that most of us haven't had as much opportunity to learn listening skills as we have for some of the other communication skills. We take listening for granted, assuming that if we can hear, we can listen well. Speaking and writing are taught, but listening usually is not. We take literature and composition classes to help us express ourselves in writing. Most of us have had at least one speech class in high school or college. Or we join Toastmasters or some other organization to help us become better at public speaking. But we seldom get any formal training in listening. That lack of training handicaps us in our most important business and personal relationships.

Benefits of Becoming a Better Listener   Becoming a better listener is one of the best things you can do for your partner. It will also yield huge benefits in your business life. Listening has been called "the quiet miracle." And it is. When you listen, all kinds of wonderful things can happen in a relationship. Here are just a few:

You and your partner become closer because you hear and understand each other's point of view.

Conflicts become more manageable because you can use your understanding to help you talk things over. Differences become negotiable instead of divisive.

You both feel supported even when you disagree. And because you feel supported, you can move from disagreement to compromise.

You can manage your anger and frustration more easily because you are clear on the issues—your own as well as your partner's.

You are able to decode your partner's words because you have listened. You then can ask questions when appropriate, so you can gather the information you need to foster understanding.

You are able to give the best gift possible—your undistracted attention and attentive listening. You are telling your partner he or she matters and so does your relationship.

Listening as an Active Process   Listening is more than simply hearing. Hearing is a passive process. You just sit there and the other person's words come and go. The old cliché "it went in one ear and out the other" describes how this works. Listening, on the other hand, is an active process. If you are truly listening, you are taking in the words and interacting with them mentally. You are hearing, processing, and understanding. Your focus is on your partner, not yourself. "What is my partner saying? What does he/she mean?" are questions you are asking yourself. The other person has your attention and knows it. You face your partner, maintaining eye contact and body language that says, "I'm with you." Appropriate questions and thoughtful responses show you are indeed listening. Listening helps your interactions become true communications instead of monologues.

Think back to the last conflict you had with your partner. Chances are it could have gone better if you had used listening skills. In the following example, the couple did not use good listening skills.

Janice stormed into the room waving the joint checkbook. "We have got to get our finances under control," she said sharply. "These overdraft charges are killing us." Feeling attacked and matching her angry tone, Norm shot back, "Well, that's because you won't enter your checks as you write them. How can we keep track of anything when you are so careless?" "You're the one who bought the new camping gear," Janice responded, feeling her anger grow. From there the situation deteriorated into one of their familiar fights, complete with the usual bitter accusations. Clearly, such confrontations, with their escalating anger and accusations, were not a useful means of communication for this couple.

Here is what could have happened with the use of effective listening skills:

Janice stormed into the room waving the joint checkbook. "We have got to get our finances under control," she said sharply. "These overdraft charges are killing us." Norm took a deep breath and tried out his newly learned skills. Remembering to listen first before responding, he asked as calmly as he could, "What has happened?" "The bank just sent us a notice that we bounced another check," Janice responded. "Let's talk about what check it was and what we need to do differently," Norm said.

The problem with the bounced check was still there, but the couple was able to talk about it more calmly. From there they could go on to problem-solve. Had Norm matched Janice's anger, the usual fight would have happened. Because he listened first, he was able to open a door to a discussion and close the door to his defensiveness.

Learning to Listen   Here are some ways to learn to listen.

1. **Resolve to pay attention to what your partner is saying.** No mental vacations, no thinking of your response while your partner is speaking, no assuming you have heard it all before. Just listen. Bite your tongue or take deep breaths if you have to

and just listen. Show your partner that you are paying attention through eye contact and body language.

2. **Rehearse in your mind what you have heard.** Restate it to yourself and your partner. Saying, "So you are concerned about our credit rating when our bills are late?" allows you to make sure you understood your partner's concern. If you are confused, you can ask for clarification.

3. **Keep your response in check until you have really listened to your partner.** Reassure yourself that you will have ample opportunity to state your point of view once you have heard that of your partner.

4. **Know that listening is difficult and will take work at first.** Resolve to really hear your partner.

People working to develop their listening behavior report that they usually feel awkward and self-conscious at first. Because we are so used to snapping back with a quick response, just listening may feel strange to us. Perhaps it even feels a bit phony at first. That is the case with any new behavior we acquire. There is always an initial awkwardness coupled with a feeling of being self-conscious. As we build our skills, it becomes easier, and we tend to lose that self-consciousness. The same is true of listening—it does get easier. And it pays tremendous dividends in your relationship. In a relationship based on mutuality, the more you listen to your partner, the more you will be listened to.

Step Two: Develop Your Speaking Skills
Learning to be a good listener is only half the process of improving your communication skills. Now you are ready to add the speaking part. As with becoming a better listener, developing a more effective speaking style is difficult, but well worth the effort.

We All Have Some Bad Habits　　Poor speaking habits are as common as poor listening habits. Have you ever:

Noticed your partner's glazed eyes and realized that you had droned on too long and lost his/her attention?

Gotten into an angry, accusatory mode of speaking and turned your partner off?

Gotten into an angry, accusatory mode of speaking and lost track of what you really wanted to say?

Interrupted your partner to override what he/she was saying?

Said the wrong thing and hurt or offended your partner without meaning to?

Defended your viewpoint when simply listening would have been more helpful?

Heard your tone of voice rising in response to the anger in your partner's voice?

Gotten so focused on being right that your discussion hit a brick wall?

Speaking to be Heard—Some Strategies Being able to clearly convey your thoughts and feelings to your partner is critical if your relationship is to survive and thrive. Here are some strategies you can use to facilitate communication.

1. **Practice good listening skills.** Make sure you have heard your partner and understand the situation before opening your mouth. It has been said that we have two ears and one mouth so that we can hear twice as much as we speak. Take that saying to heart and be reminded to really listen. Think of it as the 2:1 principle of communication: listen twice as much as you speak.

2. **Think about what it is you want your partner to know.** What is the point you wish to make? How can you convey it clearly and concisely? Kay remembers a time when she was teaching a class and was enthusiastically expounding on a subject near and dear to her heart. She realized she had gone on too long when she saw the students' dazed expressions. Just then a student in the back of the room raised a hand and asked, "Can you just put that in a nutshell?" Use the nutshell technique in your dealings with your partner. Say enough to be clear, but not so much that you lose your partner's attention. You can

discuss the need to save for the children's college fund without giving a lecture on world economics.

3. **Be as specific as you can.** Generalizations can sound like accusations. They block communication and don't tell us what change needs to happen. Saying "Your spending is out of control" or "You are so stingy with money" won't facilitate the discussion. It doesn't tell your partner what needs to happen to change the situation. Instead, provide explicit information such as "We went $75 over our budget this month," or "I really would like to save enough to re-carpet the hallway by September." Your partner will respond to specifics because the information is out in the open.

4. **Avoid name-calling and labeling.** Calling your partner names like "spendthrift," "miser," or "cheapskate" is guaranteed to raise the conflict level and lower productivity. Giving your partner specific information about what you want to happen will move the conversation along; name-calling will bring it to a halt.

5. **Avoid blaming, shaming, or accusing your partner by using "I" messages.** Say "I need to talk about how we can keep better track of our bank balance" rather than "You always bounce checks," or "I am really upset that our charge card is over the limit" instead of "There you go again, spending money we don't have." Use "I" messages to keep communication clear and respectful. "You" messages usually are hurtful and unproductive. Hurtful pronunciations have a way of stopping communication in its tracks.

6. **Watch your tone of voice if you want to be heard.** When your voice becomes loud or angry, your partner will probably hear the harsh tone, instead of your words. Make a conscious effort to keep your voice at a conversational level. Lower your voice and your partner will probably do the same. Both of you will benefit, because the discussion will remain focused on the issues at hand rather than the anger.

7. **Keep the past out of it.** Assume you both are starting fresh and don't dredge up old hurts and wrongdoing. You can't

change that situation from two years ago, you can only learn from it and move on. If you find yourself obsessing on a past hurt, you may need to get some outside help from a counselor, therapist, or spiritual advisor. Resolve to stay in the present as much as possible. That will help your discussions remain productive and fruitful.

8. **Focus on solving joint problems, not on being right.** Nobody wins in a power struggle. Anger, accusations, blaming, and shaming are relationship dead ends. Negotiating and building consensus lead to increased trust and ongoing growth. Keep your attention on the problem and resist trying to prove your partner wrong. Your goal in communication is to solve a problem. If you keep this goal in mind, you will find the discussion stays on track and yields positive results.

9. **Be willing to take a time-out.** If you hit an impasse in your discussion, or feel anger rising, it probably means that you both need a break. Agree to stop for now and return to the topic at a specified time. You will be better able to communicate after a break because you both will be rested and refreshed. And you may find that the tension has dissipated, leading to a discussion that generates solutions to problems.

10. **Take time to appreciate each other.** Sometimes couples get so focused on what is going wrong that they forget to acknowledge the positive changes that are happening. A little appreciation of progress made can do wonders to encourage you both in your efforts to work together. Telling your partner, "I really like the way we have been working together to pay off the credit cards" is encouraging and gives you both a needed pat on the back. Encouragement also provides you with the incentive to keep working on your issues. Remember that your relationship is worth the effort.

Like learning to listen, speaking clearly and to the point may feel a bit awkward at first. Using "I" messages and other communication strategies may seem cumbersome and hard to remember. Again, we encourage you to give these methods a fair trial and give yourself the opportunity to learn these new skills. The rewards of having open, comfortable discussions about money issues will foster growth and love in your relationship. Money discussions don't have to be filled with anger and anxiety.

COLLABORATIVE PROBLEM SOLVING AND REACHING CONSENSUS

Once you become comfortable putting these listening and speaking skills into practice, you are ready to move on to the next step— reaching consensus in problem solving. Here are some steps to follow.

1. **Define the problem in terms of needs.** What do you each need in the situation? Notice we are saying needs, not possible solutions. When couples focus on solutions at the beginning of the process, they risk having the discussion end up being a debate about whose solution to implement. List your needs to begin with.

   Dale and Jan were into their usual struggle about their finances. They had spent many hours arguing about how much to save each month. Focusing on which amount was "right" led to seemingly endless arguments. Once they began to focus on needs, however, the issue became clearer. Jan had a high need for security. She saw a savings plan as a hedge against future uncertainty. Dale was more concrete in his needs. He saw savings as a way of paying for a new car and the house remodeling they had planned on. Once they understood each other's needs, they were able to find a compromise plan that worked for both of them.

2. **Brainstorm to come up with solutions that will meet both persons' needs.** Again, we remind you to let the solutions flow from the needs. For Jan and Dale, thinking up potential need-based solutions led to a productive discussion about their future. Each came up with solutions that met the needs they listed. Jan and Dale decided to split their savings. They had

one saving plan for the long-term future and another for shorter-term purchases and projects.

3. **Select the solution that will best meet the needs of both parties.** You may wish to combine solutions. Jan and Dale found that they could put the short-term savings into one fund and invest the long-term savings in another. As part of their solution, they also decided who was going to be responsible for finding the appropriate ways to invest their money. Jan would deal with the short-term savings while Dale would investigate a place to put their long-term funds.

4. **Evaluate the plan and revise if necessary.** Jan and Dale agreed to implement their plan for the following three months. At the end of that period they could then see how their plan was working and change it if necessary. Because they both felt good about the cooperative spirit they were able to generate, savings became a joint challenge rather than a bone of contention. They eagerly looked forward to tracking the progress of their investments and reminded each other of how this was beneficial to them as a couple.

As you put these four steps into place, keep your focus on the issue in front of you. Don't allow yourselves to be sidetracked by fighting over who is right. Your goal is to cooperate, not win. Seeing progress as you solve your shared problems will encourage you to keep trying. And the new spirit of cooperation will strengthen your relationship as a couple.

WHAT TO DO IF YOU NEED ADDITIONAL HELP

Old patterns can be hard to break. Sometimes couples find they need some extra help to get back on track and learn to communicate better. There are several routes you can follow if this is the case for you.

You may wish to seek couples therapy. Your local telephone directory will have a listing of therapists who work with couples. You can also contact the American Association for Marriage and Family Therapy for a referral in your community. If you choose to see a therapist, make sure the person you select feels competent to work with your issues regarding the subject of money. A recent survey of marital therapists found that 43 percent expressed doubts about their ability to intervene with couples struggling with money issues.[1]

Another approach would be to take a class. Some of the better-known marriage education programs focus on helping couples develop better communication skills.[2] While this is not an all-inclusive list, here are some programs for you to consider:

Practical Application of Relationship Skills (PAIRS). A family therapist developed this program to help couples learn communication skills in a structured course setting. In PAIRS courses, couples learn techniques to help them communicate in a caring, effective manner. The opportunity to look at family-of-origin issues and how they affect the couple is also provided. Participants leave the class with a series of tools to use in their relationship.

Couples Communication. This was one of the earliest couples education programs. The course uses body movement as well as intellectual learning as part of its format. The course helps couples systematically review inner information (thoughts, feelings, wants, sensory data, and actions) that can influence problems they confront. Participants learn to use the program's techniques to help them deal with conflicts in their relationship.

Prevention and Relationship Enhancement Program (PREP). This program helps couples set up ground rules for conflict. PREP works within a structured format to help couples utilize their differences productively.

Relationship Enhancement (RE). Empathy is the starting point of this program. Each partner learns to see things from the other's point of view. Empathic listening and learning to express viewpoints in a way that fosters communication are highlights of RE.

Marriage Survival Kit. John Gottman, a noted marriage researcher, developed this program, which utilizes some of his research findings. He helps couples focus on their everyday dealings in order to learn more about each other so that they can handle conflicts better.

Financial Peace University. This 13-week program is specifically geared to helping couples straighten out their money issues. Couples learn about financial management strategies as well other relationship issues.

If you decide to take a class to strengthen your relationship as a couple, your choice will be as individual as you are. No one class fits for every couple; this list is to give you some ideas of what is available. We cannot make a specific recommendation. Your individual interests, couple dynamics, the time you are willing to invest, and the money you can spend for such training will influence your choice. For that reason, it is important that you spend some time investigating these and other formal classes to pick the one that is best suited to your needs as a couple. Also keep in mind that many churches and synagogues offer classes for members of their community. These classes may be an excellent fit for you.

A FINAL WORD OF ENCOURAGEMENT

Learning to communicate about your money issues may well be one of the most difficult tasks you face as a couple. Take the amount of emotional baggage you bring into a relationship from your past, add the fear, stress, and misplaced priorities about money in general, throw in society's prohibitions against discussing it, and you are facing a major challenge. You are also being given a great opportunity. Developing clear couples communication skills and applying them to the issue of money can empower your relationship in important ways. As you learn to talk about one of the most emotion-laden issues in our society with mutual respect, caring, and honesty, your bond becomes stronger. When you face your money anxieties together, you build trust and confidence. Clearly communicating your needs, fears, anxieties, hopes, and dreams results in a shared experience that is the basis for a lasting relationship.

Our belief in writing this book is that you *can* work through your money issues. You can learn to communicate. And you can use your improved communication skills to heal old wounds, develop new trust, and move through your lives together with increased love and understanding. We invite you to begin this most important process.

MOVING FORWARD ▶▶▶▶▶▶▶▶

This chapter provides specific suggestions couples can use to improve their money-communication skills. We believe that developing clear communication is one of the most important steps you can take to move your relationship toward more productive discussions about your money issues. As an added benefit, improved communication skills will strengthen your relationship and make it more fulfilling in all areas. The time you invest in learning these skills will pay huge dividends.

Here are some steps you can take immediately to develop better money-communication skills. Once you become comfortable discussing money, you can transfer your newfound skills to other areas of your relationship.

1. Write down the last disagreement you and your partner had about money. Write as if you are a reporter for a newspaper. Leave the emotion out of it and write only what would be observable to a bystander.

2. Analyze the interaction as objectively as possible. Pinpoint where effective speaking and listening skills could have been used. How might their use have changed the direction of the disagreement?

3. Rewrite the disagreement using the principles of speaking and listening outlined in this chapter.

4. Practice your speaking and listening skills in other areas of your relationship. They will come more easily as you continue to use them.

12

WRITING NEW MESSAGES

So far we've asked you to drag a virtual ploughshare through your beliefs and behaviors involving money. At the same time, we have suggested many couples activities for you to tackle and recommended numerous meetings between you and your partner so you can openly and safely reveal what you have learned about yourself and your money messages. Following through with all these activities has probably been challenging at times, but we know how effective they are in helping you develop the healthy relationship you both want with money and with each other. You have been encouraged to separate your emotions from your money messages as much as possible so that talking about them is easier. After all, our emotional investment in our belief system is what keeps those messages intact. So when we're exploring which beliefs work for our benefit and which ones don't, separating out our emotional ties enables us to objectively challenge our money-related convictions and at the same time evaluate their effectiveness.

What we will be asking you to accomplish in this chapter has more power to change your relationship with money and each other than any other single chapter in this book. You'll be designing what you want to believe, not what you want to achieve. We will discuss external goals in Chapter 14. Our current focus is on the internal truths that you can now freely choose and that will form the foundation for your relationship with money. What you decide upon here, both individually and together, has the power to change your experiences involving money. The new messages you develop will affect your future together and will help to form your children's relationship with money. For those of you in business together, you are developing a corporate culture that will affect your business and your employees.

DESIGNING NEW MESSAGES

You have already experienced the power of your belief system, most of which was developed unconsciously. So you know the importance of bringing awareness to the process of deciding exactly what you want your new beliefs to be. A certain amount of caution needs to be exercised as you develop the wording for those messages you want to embrace. We will give you guidelines to follow throughout this process, along with methods for implanting your desired messages into your psyche. There's certainly an aura of seriousness about what we will do in this chapter. That said, we encourage you both to have fun with the upcoming activities. This is the time to give your creativity full rein, and creativity flourishes amid fun and joy.

Now we are ready to begin designing new beliefs related to money. We urge you to work out your individual messages first, then work together to develop new shared beliefs. You may discover that some of your newly designed individual money messages are exactly what your partner needs as well. Great! You may also learn that your shared affirmations are slightly different from your individual ones. That's fine, too. We ask you to restrict yourself to a total of three to five new beliefs, whether individual or shared, so we're not talking large numbers of redesigned convictions. Attempting to work with any more than that overwhelms your psyche to the point that no change will happen. Money beliefs don't have to be complex and convoluted. Usually three to five core statements cover all aspects of how we want to relate to money.

Beliefs + Behaviors

Each partner should begin with his or her personal beliefs concerning money. Ask yourselves, "What messages do I want to hear inside my head? What kinds of behaviors do I want to result from those beliefs?" Internal messages and behaviors are absolutely linked, so redesigning messages means different behaviors will result. Suppose one message you have identified tells you "Money is dirty and people who want and have money are greedy." The behavior derived from this message is to get rid of any extra money you have. So when you have money left over from paying your bills, you rationalize your good bill-paying by buying yourself something—a new article of clothing, something for the house, a new gadget. You do anything that will rid yourself of any extra money. You won't invest it because then you might have even more of the filthy stuff.

But now you're with a partner who does save and invest. And you are realizing your message and its accompanying behavior do you more harm than good. So you may decide that a more appropriate message might be "Having savings and investments gives me the financial stability I want" or "I define what money is in my life" or whatever message addresses your core issue, redesigns it to suit your desired relationship with money, and supports behaviors you want regarding money.

Perhaps it's more appropriate for you to ask those questions in the reverse order—"What new behaviors do I want? What beliefs will support those behaviors?" For example, if you tend to be anxious about money, one behavior you might like to change is always worrying and feeling powerless about your financial situation. What's the underlying message of such behavior? As we have already explored, the same behavior can have a variety of underlying beliefs, depending upon an individual's experience. Worry might come from such beliefs as "I need someone else to take care of me financially" or "I don't know how to take care of myself financially" or "I don't have enough money and I never will," among other possibilities. Depending upon the underlying message, you might want to replace the anxiety with confidence or with the knowledge that you do take care of yourself financially or by deeply embracing the notion of abundance. Your new message might be "I am confident and powerful with money" or "I take care of myself financially" or "I am a part of the abundance of the universe."

Choosing the Language

The language for your new beliefs must be chosen carefully. Make certain you use words that have the meaning you want to convey and that don't carry any negative or unwanted connotations for you. For example, don't use the word "higher" if you are afraid of heights, even when you are referring to something other than elevation. Your subconscious responds to a long-held belief associated with the word "higher" and reacts with fear when it hears that reference. Even the word "abundance" has many differing meanings for people. Avoid descriptions that are too general, such as "good" or "a lot." The more specific, the better. Working these new beliefs out on paper is helpful, as is doing this activity with your partner. Often others can spot potentially confusing or misleading wording that we don't see.

Always use present tense to convey the assurance to your entire psyche that your new belief is firmly in place. If you use future tense, the belief will never take hold because as far as the subconscious is concerned, only present time exists. In one of the examples above, we have used the wording "I take care of myself financially" rather than "I *can* take care of myself financially." The word "can" implies some amount of uncertainty and is simply unnecessary. Our deeply held beliefs are certain—that's why they have so much power in determining our behavior.

When designing your new messages, remember to limit yourself to just three to five. That's plenty to work with, and most people can distill their essential money beliefs into just a few well-crafted statements.

ACCEPTING YOUR NEW BELIEF

Words alone are not enough. We have emphasized the tie between beliefs and feelings every time we've asked you to separate the two during your discussions with each other. The feelings associated with a belief are what hold that message in place within your entire belief system and give it power in your life. So when looking at money beliefs that no longer serve you, stepping back from the feelings tied to them is appropriate. On the other hand, when you are developing new convictions, tying these messages to the feelings you want to have when you call up the belief is essential. Without the feelings, the new message you have designed will fail to take hold in your belief system.

Beliefs + Feelings

The next logical question is "How do I know how I will feel? My new message isn't imbedded into my belief system yet." If you had never experienced the feeling accompanying the new belief, the message would not have occurred to you in the first place. Somewhere in your psyche, you have felt the feeling you want to capture with your new message. It may or may not have been associated with money. What the desired feeling is currently associated with is irrelevant. You are going to create the critical link between the feeling and your new belief. At this stage of our work with couples, we generally encourage people to simply get out of their own way and allow their vast reservoir of feelings to provide them with the appropriate support for this next step.

Taking a look at your new messages, choose one that you want to work with first. You will focus on this one message until it becomes a part of your belief system before moving on to another new conviction. For this part of the process, select a time when you will not be interrupted. While focusing on your desired message, ask yourself, "How do I feel when I say this message to myself, knowing that it is true?" Allow plenty of time for a feeling to arise within you. Or recall a time when you had the feeling you want to have with the new message. What kinds of feelings do you want your new belief to evoke? Security? Peacefulness? Joy? Strength? When did you have these feelings? It doesn't matter that the sense of being peaceful came during your last massage, or that any of the feelings you want came from some event other than one associated with money.

Once you have recalled the feeling, allow yourself to experience it fully. Close your eyes to block out external distractions so you can fully focus on your inner experience. Let the sense of peacefulness or strength or safety or whatever feeling you have chosen run through your entire body, head to toe to fingertips. When your body feels full of this chosen emotion, repeat your new message over and over to yourself until the two are firmly linked.

Now open your eyes, get up and walk around, saying your new conviction out loud. Do you respond with the desired feelings? If not, repeat the activity until you automatically have the feeling you want to have when you state your new message. Repeat the new declaration as often as you can—in the shower, while doing any kind of physical activity, and especially if the old message rears its head. Write it down and post it where you will see it frequently throughout the day. The bathroom mirror and refrigerator are favorite places. We also recommend laying a note card with the message in a desk drawer that you open often during the day. Write it on pieces of paper that you put into your wallet with your paper money and in your checkbook so that you see it each time you open them. By crafting words that resonate with you and by associating them with the feelings you want to experience, you are doubly reinforcing the new belief. This combination is powerful and will enable you to create a more satisfactory money-related belief system than the one you may currently have.

How Long Will It Take?

Exactly how long the process of fully accepting your new belief will take depends upon many factors, all of them subjective. The strength of the old belief can make a difference, as can how deeply imbedded it is in your belief system. Giving yourself a few moments to feel the feeling you have associated with your new conviction each time you say it quickens the process. So does repeating your new belief many times throughout the day, even saying it before you fall asleep and when you awaken. It's even a good substitute for some of the things people say about other drivers while driving. The next time someone does something with their car that you wish they hadn't, repeat your new money belief out loud several times instead of making comments about that driver's parentage. You will feel much better, and you will be making great progress toward developing your desired relationship with money.

At some point in this process, you will hear yourself say your new message and your entire being will respond with a feeling of acceptance. You will know with your head and your body that you firmly believe what you have just said. The behavior you wanted as an outgrowth of the chosen belief will feel natural to you. It may feel so comfortable that you may not even notice your behaviors changing. Perhaps your partner or friends will notice your new behavior before you realize you've changed. Most, probably not all, of the struggle in this part of your relationship with money is gone. These are all signs that your new belief is in place and you can move to the next one.

SHARED BELIEFS

So far we have focused on your individual messages and the process for refining them. This is because we have to be clear within ourselves before we can attempt to create shared money beliefs with our partner. Conflicts tend to arise within relationships because of contradicting belief systems, and this state is fed by individuals who are unclear about exactly what they believe. By working out your individual money messages and gaining clarity with them, you have eliminated this potentially devastating situation.

Another reason we ask you to develop new beliefs for yourself before approaching this issue with your partner is to increase the likelihood that each of you will have your needs met in your shared messages. When we are clear about the beliefs we want to have operating in our lives and the kind of relationship we want with money, then as we develop shared convictions, we are less likely to settle or give in, agreeing to a notion that we cannot truly embrace. Getting caught in this trap is disastrous for the process of developing shared beliefs, since the person who feels compromised will resent the entire activity. She or he will feel deprived and resentful. These feelings can then get buried under rationalizations only to surface in subtly sabotaging behaviors.

After your new individual money beliefs are firmly in place, the two of you can be working out new tenets you want for your relationship. The same questions about beliefs and behaviors are relevant. "What new messages involving money do we want to embrace as partners? What behaviors are likely to result?" The new beliefs the two of you design may be similar to or even the same as one or more of your individual beliefs. Or they may be different. They cannot be oppositional or nothing is going to change. With input from both partners, work out the wording for your shared beliefs. Then choose one you both want to develop first. Talk about the feelings you each want to associate with this message, realizing that they may be different for each of you. Pull up the feelings you want, just as you did with your individual beliefs, and link the message with the emotion. Follow the same techniques for imbedding the shared belief that you did for the individual ones. With both of you focusing your energy on the same conviction, you are creating a powerful force for redesigning your shared relationship with money as well as with each other.

We have urged you to stick with one message at a time so that you don't overwhelm your psyche. The same suggestion applies when you are working on shared beliefs. You will get to all of your shared messages eventually, so the most important thing is to get started and follow through with the commitment you have made to yourself and to your partner.

HAVE SOME FUN

See if you can have some fun with this entire process. We have suggested writing out your new message and posting it in strategic places where you will be reminded of it frequently. Try using your computer to create some interesting-looking reminders. Perhaps you may want to add clip art that reminds you of the feeling you have associated with the message. Colored text might grab your attention. One client carried his new message in his golf bag, printed on a half sheet of paper beside a picture of a golfer teeing off. His accompanying mental image was of him making a hole in one as a result of his drive to accept his new message. One picture carried many words for him and he associated his money message with an activity that was relaxing and enjoyable.

Another client designed her message with pictures of trees and birds to remind her of the peaceful feelings she gets when she is enjoying nature. She wanted those calm sensations associated with her money message. Among other places, she taped the message and picture to the center of her steering wheel. She told us that not only did the words and picture help her accept her new money belief, but being constantly reminded of her desired feelings also encouraged her to be a more relaxed driver—an added bonus!

One couple asked their close family members and friends to help celebrate their new messages and threw a party once they had decided on exactly what the new beliefs would be. They hung banners adorned with the new statements and illustrations that represented the desired associated feelings and posted them throughout their home. They specifically asked for their loved ones' support and for their acknowledgement of the effort the two had put into working toward a new relationship with money. This couple viewed their work as a commitment to a deeper level in their relationship with each other, and they wanted to make this important step public just as they had made their commitment to each other public during their wedding ceremony. They noted that some of their friends seemed uncomfortable at first with such an open exposure of their money beliefs. But as the secrecy so often associated with money evaporated during the gathering, so did many of their guests' inhibitions about discussing money issues. This shift, they told us, was fascinating to experience.

While such a public announcement—even if it was to a select group of loved ones—is unusual, the point this couple made is worth reinforcing. Working out money issues and agreeing to develop shared money beliefs that will serve each of you individually and as a couple is a major step in committing to a deeper relationship with each other. You are both acknowledging that together you can build the kind of life you want and/or the kind of business you want. Individually we each have the power to do just that. Together, our power becomes exponentially greater.

MOVING FORWARD ▶ ▶ ▶ ▶ ▶ ▶ ▶ ▶

Designing and believing your individual and shared new money beliefs forms the basis for a healthy new relationship with money. These steps get you where you want to go. First apply them to yourselves individually, then work through them together.

1. Answer these questions: "What messages do I want to hear inside my head? What kinds of behaviors do I want to result from those beliefs?"

2. Write out three to five messages, carefully choosing the language: know the exact meanings of the words, use present tense, be specific.

3. Tie each message to the feelings you want to have, anchoring them in your body.

4. Display the message you're working with in places where you will be reminded of it frequently.

5. Work with one message at a time until you feel and know it is true for you.

DEVELOPING A NEW VISION

E ach of us right now is living the way we live, working where we work, being in partnership with a particular person, because of the vision we have held for ourselves, whether we have been aware of that image or not. Some aspects of our lives may be more obviously connected to our vision than others are. You may have started out some years ago by imagining yourself doing a particular kind of work, and that mental picture produced the excitement, energy, interest, curiosity, or whatever you needed to steadily move toward realizing your vision. With this motivating force you may have gone to college and majored in a certain field so that you could have the career that you have now. Or you may have started out at the proverbial ground floor and worked your way into your current job. A strong vision can generate the kind of energy you need to accomplish difficult tasks, learn challenging material, take risks, or simply make your way through some boring classes required for the degree that will move you closer to fulfilling that desire. In other words, you are currently living the vision you have had for yourself up to this point, just as all of us are. This vision includes your partner, just as you are included in your partner's vision.

As with many other money-related discussions, developing a shared vision requires that you delve into the subject with probing questions. In this case, it's appropriate to ask each other, "Do you see what I see?"

WHAT IS A VISION?
In understanding exactly what a vision is, it's important to also know what it isn't. Your vision is the sum total of how you want to live your life. It covers everything, including how you want to earn money,

where you want to live, what kind of home you want, the relationship you want with your partner, your children, even your pets. Your vision includes how you want to feel when you get up, how you want to feel during the day and at the end of the day, every day. Your vision is the big picture of your life and everything about your life.

While this book focuses on you and your partner's relationship with money, isolating your vision for money from everything else is unrealistic. Money is tied to most aspects of the vision. Even when we talk about how you want to feel about your life overall and about the specifics that make up your vision, we are also including feelings about money. Every aspect of our vision is linked to every other part.

Misconceptions

Sometimes when we are explaining the nature of a vision, someone in the group will say, "Oh, it's our daydreams and fantasies." This is a common misconception. A fantasy usually belongs to the realm of fiction and serves to entertain or otherwise distract us from present-day reality. Fantasies can be quite healthy when we keep in mind that they serve us as a way to relax or even gain some needed distance from a problem. Generally speaking, fantasies are best left unfulfilled—reality rarely measures up to our unleashed imagination. Daydreams, on the other hand, may include fantasies as well as more realistic ideas about our desires. But for most people they are still primarily fantasies—maybe they could happen, but probably they won't. There's no commitment to a fantasy. When we decide that we are going to consciously create a new vision that includes some or all of the elements of our dreams, then the dream becomes part of our vision. Taking this step moves us toward making the dream a reality in our life. Our vision is our intention for the totality of our lives that we satisfy in varying degrees every day. Later in this chapter, we will discuss how to use your daydream time to help you implement your vision.

Another common misconception concerning the vision is that it is the same thing as a goal. Our goals arise from our vision, becoming the steps we take to realize the vision. So they are linked. Understanding this connection is important to your overall success in redesigning your relationship with money. This is why we place the vision chapter before the goals chapter in this book. Goals that are unconnected to a vision are inherently difficult, if not impossible, to achieve; while they may sound good, they lack the inspiration that goals connected to our vision naturally have. Our vision is the fertile ground from which our goals grow.

The Vision's Organic Nature

We deliberately use the fertile-soil analogy because a vision is an organic part of our lives. Rather than being carved in stone, the vision expands, contracts, and changes as we mature, in a lifelong process of constantly recreating ourselves. The vision we have for ourselves in our twenties is usually very different from the one we have in our fifties. We fine-tune our vision to reflect how we are and how we want to be in the world as well as within ourselves. Life experience leads to shifts in our vision throughout our lives. And our partner, whether a life partner or business partner, is likewise functioning with his or her vision. Developing a shared vision is critical as the two of you create the kind of shared relationship with money that you want.

BELIEFS, VALUES, AND VISION

As you have probably figured out, our inner messages and values play a huge part in shaping our vision. Our beliefs about ourselves largely determine whether or not we can see or vividly imagine ourselves living the kind of life we say we want to live and having the relationship with money that we think we want. As the old saying tells us, "If you can see it and believe it, you can achieve it." We've done a lot of work so far on the "believing it" part—redesigning deeply held beliefs, shining a light on values, reevaluating money messages and getting rid of the ones that are no longer useful. Both of you have designed shared messages and begun implementing them so that they are becoming imbedded in your psyches as individuals and as a couple. Now your shared vision is ready to arise quite naturally from your new beliefs. It's time to embrace the "seeing it" part.

As you proceed through this chapter, place your newly clarified values and message statements nearby so you can refer to them. We could argue that beliefs come first, followed by the vision, just as successfully as we could argue that the vision precedes the beliefs. But this chicken-or-egg question is really a moot point for our purposes here. You already have a strong foundation for your vision in the form of your redesigned messages, so now we want to allow your shared vision to arise from all the inner work you have both accomplished up to this point.

You probably have a fairly clear idea of what your current vision consists of, given your extensive exploration of your currently held beliefs. So we're going to skip any attempt to uncover the details of your existing vision in favor of directing your energy toward creating a new one. Granted, it may contain elements of your current vision— that will become apparent as you move forward with this process. What we will focus on is the picture you both want to carry with you from this point forward. Your vision lives simultaneously in the present moment as well as in the future. It can envelop you today while seducing you toward tomorrow. The joy of having a shared vision is found in consciously creating the life or the business you want to share with your partner.

WORKING TOGETHER

One concern we have in using the word "vision" to describe the overall concept you have for your life is that you will believe that you must literally *see* your vision. Those of you who are naturally good at visualizing will undoubtedly use your abilities in this area to facilitate the process of developing a vision. But those readers who never see vivid pictures when daydreaming or doing relaxation or guided-imagery exercises, take heart! You are, in all likelihood, a kinesthetic individual, which means that you learn by doing, or you learn through physical (kinetic) activity. So while you may not see things internally, you sense them physically. You learn best by hands-on doing rather than by reading about how to do something. We will suggest some activities to accommodate this particular learning style. Others learn auditorially—they best learn things by hearing about them. Talking out loud about the vision you are creating, putting all the elements into words and describing and discussing those with your partner enhances the auditory learning process.

As you and your partner develop your shared vision, we are going to ask that you involve as many senses as you can. Incorporating your visual, auditory, and kinesthetic (body) senses speeds the learning process and deepens the entire experience. As you create your shared vision, we urge you to use your collective creativity to see, hear, and feel your vision. For fun, try adding in smell and taste as well. We will make suggestions for facilitating this experience.

Respecting Different Approaches
When starting an activity as extensive as building a shared vision, respect for each other's approach to the task is paramount. We want to discuss two distinctly different, but equally valid, techniques, just in case you and your partner have opposite styles. When creating something new, some people need to see the whole picture first, then break out the pieces. Others use just the reverse approach, getting a grasp on the details, then allowing the total image to emerge from a synthesis of these parts.

If you and your partner each use different styles, we suggest that you begin independently working out what you would like to have in a shared vision. There's a very simple reason for this suggestion.

When two people have potentially conflicting approaches to a shared task—one starting with the whole picture and the other beginning with the details—they can quickly become distracted from their purpose and end up in a confusing power struggle over whose technique is the "right" one. The person who needs the details first can easily get lost in the other's descriptions of the big picture. Lacking the details, the partner experiences the large view as empty, since the details build the whole picture for this person. Frustration with both his or her partner and the activity is soon to follow. Conversely, the big-picture person can become bogged down in listening to his or her partner's detailed descriptions. Without the whole picture, this individual cannot mentally organize the details, so they can flutter about in meaningless disconnection. Once this struggle between styles happens, your shared vision can seem impossible to develop.

If you're not sure how your partner would approach this activity, ask him or her, "Do you need the details first to get to the whole picture, or the picture, then the details?" If the two of you have been together for any length of time and have tried to engage in problem solving activities, you probably both already know the answer to this question!

Making It Click

If you have differing styles, we urge you not to dump your preferred way of handling this project. You might be tempted to rationalize that it would save time if you both just worked on it together at the outset. But the person whose natural style is not being used will likely struggle unnecessarily with an unfamiliar, even uncomfortable, approach and be distracted from the intent of the activity. By not using your familiar method at the outset, you may also fail to get something you want included in the vision. When this happens, resentment will set in and your shared vision will be neither shared nor a viable vision. If you both use the same approach, great! Then you can develop your shared vision together at the outset. But if you have different approaches, do your part separately from your partner, each of you developing the details and the overall vision in the order that makes sense to you. Once you have both of these key elements—the specifics and the entire vision—you are ready to bring your ideas together so that both individual visions becomes melded together into a shared whole.

CREATING YOUR VISION

We are going to suggest several activities to help make your shared vision concrete. A natural place to start is by building on the new beliefs and values you have been putting into practice. Then we will put form to your vision and finally explore ways to implement your shared view so that you can both begin living your vision.

Reading over your reconstructed values and newly designed messages, allow a picture or sense of your vision to begin forming. How do you want your life to be, especially your relationship with money? Think about the totality of your life and the role you want money to play. Let all sorts of ideas and possibilities float around, even if they seem preposterous. Sometimes our outrageous thoughts give rise to more realistic, creative notions. As these ideas, pictures, or sensations arise, begin writing them down. Phrases that capture the essence of a feeling and/or thought are fine; try not to get distracted by trying to write complete sentences. For some people, free-form brainstorming works—simply write down what occurs to you, regardless of whether it makes sense or not. Once all ideas seem to be exhausted, then the evaluation process can begin, and you can decide what to include and what to eliminate.

If you like a bit more organization than the brainstorming technique requires, you may want to write down major areas that would be included in your vision. You might use headings such as "Relationship with Money," "Characteristics of the Work I Do to Generate Money," "How I Want to Feel First Thing in the Morning and as I Am Falling Asleep at Night," and any other general category you want to address when developing your vision. Then jot down the ideas and feelings that come to you in each of these parts of your life, eventually pulling them together into a complete picture. You may discover that you currently have some pieces of your vision realized. Great! Be sure to incorporate those parts and continue building on what you already have.

The Whole Picture
Now that you have the words that describe all aspects of your shared vision, together the two of you can literally draw a picture of what it looks like. Start with a piece of heavy newsprint or construction paper and lots of different colored crayons, pencils, markers, pastels, or whatever medium invites you to play with this creation. You might take turns drawing different aspects of your vision, or, if the paper is big enough, you might draw at the same time. If one of you is much better at drawing than the other, then we suggest you both draw with your nondominant hands. This approach eliminates expectations and concerns about your artistic performance. Each of you needs to participate in creating the drawing, regardless of your skill level. This is, after all, a shared vision. For you to both have a vested interest in your vision, you need to participate in all aspects of creating it. If you are artistically challenged (we can identify with this condition), make a collage by cutting the appropriate pictures out of magazines and gluing them onto heavy paper or cardboard.

Representing feelings can be challenging to the imagination, so we suggest using colors or even an abstract image that represents the emotions you want to feel as part of your vision. For example, suppose a part of your shared vision is that you will both feel grateful to have the money to pay bills. So the person who writes out the checks as well as his or her partner both need to remind themselves to feel gratitude when paying bills or even when thinking about them. But how do you represent gratitude in your vision? Does a color or image come to mind? Choose something that has meaning to both of you, so that when you see that representation in your overall picture, you will both be reminded to feel gratitude.

Making It Tangible
The idea in creating the picture or collage is to make your shared vision as tangible as possible. You may find that you have already realized some parts of it. Be sure to include those elements in the picture you are making. That helps reinforce the fact that attaining this vision is both possible and worthwhile.

On the other hand, don't be concerned if your vision seems incomplete. We will discuss goals in the next chapter, so don't get bogged down in thinking you have to know exactly how you are going to fill in any gaps or even how you are going to make your vision a reality. What's important at this point is to have a reasonably clear picture of your shared vision—what it looks like and how it feels in all its aspects.

You may want to leave the picture or collage you've been working on lying out where you both can look at it during the next few days, keeping an eye out for anything that might need to be added or adjusted. Remember, this is a shared vision, so consult your partner and make sure you agree before actually changing anything. Once you both feel that the vision you have constructed adequately portrays how you want to be in all areas of your life or business with each other, post the picture or collage where you can see it often.

Talk about it with your partner. We often suggest that when couples get together at the end of the workday, they discuss what they did during the day to energize their vision. This focus provides something positive to talk about, reinforces every action, thought, or feeling each person has taken to support the vision, and strengthens the shared nature of your life together. Business partners can have the same discussion at the end of their day together. We're not talking huge chunks of time for this talk, five minutes might be adequate. The point is, the more energy you both put into your vision, the more life it will have.

REINFORCING YOUR VISION

All these activities reinforce your vision and help implant it into your psyche. Remind yourself of how you said you wanted to feel upon awakening in the morning and going to sleep at night. Or at the beginning of your workday and at the end of it. If you don't have those feelings immediately, then call them forth. Don't get up until you feel the way you want to feel. Start working only after you have captured the feelings you want to have about your work. Revisit them periodically throughout the day. Don't let yourself end your day until you feel the way you have described in your vision.

Sometimes getting to the desired feelings takes some effort and sometimes it seems to happen quickly. As we discussed when restructuring your beliefs, feelings are integral to making your efforts tangible. Every time you realize you're not feeling the way you want to and you make the effort to change that, you are moving closer to living out your vision. If you and your partner support each other, you can shift your vision into a reality that you are both living.

Another highly effective technique for implanting and implementing your vision involves using some of your daydreaming time to play out your vision. Everyone daydreams—it's part of the healthy functioning of the human brain. Much of this activity is devoted to entertaining fantasies that we don't expect to fulfill. Some people do a lot of "what if" and "if only" and "by golly, the next time I'll . . ." fuming during their daydreaming time. This type of thinking only drags down an individual, feeding the negativity in his or her life. It triggers the stress reaction in the body that can be measured by simple biofeedback devices. Many years ago, when Diane was teaching a basic college psychology class, she had invited another counselor to the class to demonstrate the uses of biofeedback. After hooking Diane's index finger to a simple gauge, her guest speaker asked her to think about some recent event that had made her angry. Within a second or two, the needle on the gauge flew from a flat resting position to three-quarters of the way across the gauge. This vivid demonstration of the effect of our thoughts on our physiology serves as a reminder to be cautious about what we think.

With this information in mind, you may be inspired to use your daydreaming time as an aid in making your shared vision a reality. We're not suggesting that you eliminate all your imaginary entertainment, just substitute your vision for some of that time. When you daydream your vision, you might imagine living out parts of your vision or the whole concept. For example, you might imagine yourself going through a morning routine of activities that incorporate feelings, activities, and thoughts that you and your partner want to have relating to money. As we discussed earlier, use as many senses as you can during this daydream time. See yourself and your partner involved in your vision, hear conversations, feel the emotions you want, smell the air, and taste the food. (Eating good food is a part of your vision, isn't it?)

Remembering your intention is important to using your daydream time in this manner. Your shared vision started to become your reality the moment the two of you created it. Everything you do that puts energy into it moves your vision closer to fulfillment. Your vision daydreaming needs to be accomplished with the inner assurance that it is helping you realize what you and your partner want. If you approach the daydream activity with the notion that "this is just wishful thinking" or any other thought or feeling that dismisses both the process and your vision, your energy will be wasted. The daydream energy that you can put into your vision is powerful. Just as Diane's body quickly responded to a memory about anger, so, too, will your body respond to the positive images you nurture about your shared vision. This kind of effort literally sets up your entire being to fulfill the vision you have designed. We are reminded of the old warning to be careful what you wish for—you may get it! Using the techniques we have outlined in this chapter, you and your partner will realize your shared vision.

MOVING FORWARD ▶▶▶▶▶▶▶▶

Our purpose in this chapter is to help you to develop and implement a shared vision. Pulling together everything you have done so far in this book will make implementing the following process meaningful and fun. Do this together.

1. Have your prioritized values list (Chapter 7) and your newly designed messages (Chapter 12) in front of you.

2. Involve all your senses—visual, auditory, kinesthetic (body), smell, and taste—as you design your desired vision.

3. Think about the totality of your life and the role you want money to play, writing down everything that occurs to you.

4. Draw a picture of your shared vision with as many details as you want. Be sure to include feelings.

5. Give yourselves permission to add to this picture until it feels complete.

6. Embrace your vision, feel it, daydream about it, and you will realize it.

14

GETTING THERE FROM HERE

Diane once got a fortune cookie that contained what she considered to be sage advice: "Begin from the end." She thought this suggestion wise mostly because that's the way she does things anyway. Turns out Kay does, too. What we have found over many years of working with people in a wide variety of contexts is that when it comes to goal setting, beginning from the end works best. That's essentially what we have done in the last several chapters of this book. Redesign and agree upon beliefs that you can both embrace, allow a vision for your life or business together to emerge from your new messages, and now figure out the steps you will take to realize your vision. When people try to develop goals without having a vision, those objectives become meaningless to the overall picture of their lives. They become empty wishes that have nothing to attach themselves to, often dictating to us what we *should* do, mutating into an onerous task or evolving into one more unfulfilled fantasy.

But by allowing goals to arise from a vision that is founded on the beliefs you hold most important in your relationship, they become another companion on your road to living the way you both want to, or to building the kind of business you want to be a part of. As we've suggested in previous chapters, going through this chapter will be easier if you have your new messages and vision where you can refer to them.

LET'S GET REAL

Goal setting in this culture has generally been highly overrated as *the* means to becoming successful. As we have noted, goals that are not derived from a vision have no meaning, making them very hard to accomplish. When we come to this part of our workshop and ask how many people have ever set goals, most hands go up. Then we ask how many people have set goals that they haven't realized, and once again, the majority acknowledge being part of this group. The unfortunate aspect of setting a goal, not reaching it, then setting another goal with the same unhappy outcome is the harm done to one's feeling of self-worth. We've already talked about challenges involving money and self-worth, so we don't want to add to them in urging you to set some goals. We want to be realistic about this topic.

Dump the Negatives

If you or your partner have a lot of negative messages associated with the notion of goals and goal setting, one activity that can help is finding some useful language that isn't as emotionally loaded. Goals are simply the steps, as you have defined them, that you take to build your shared vision. They are short- and long-term objectives; activities that help you move in the direction you want to go. You're in charge of their design, and with your partner's support, you can change them any time you want. We are going to try to dispel the major misconceptions people have regarding goals, so that you will start to view them as helpful companions rather than as punitive annoyances. If you have had some past experience with goals that have not served you well, now is the time to rethink how they can assist you and your partner as you move toward living your vision.

Working with the Differences

Some differences between men and women need to be noted at this point. Men tend to be more linear and step-by-step in their thinking. They enjoy the product that results from their efforts. Therefore, setting goals to be reached one at a time is generally the most comfortable approach for them. Women are generally more holistic in their thinking, able to entertain many ideas at the same time, juggling and distilling them into a whole. They enjoy the process of moving toward the realization of a task much more than the end product of that effort. In fact, women often become bored with a project just before it is completed. The process is finished even though the product may not be, so women want to move on to what is most interesting to them—the next new process. Men, in the meantime, find reward in the product and can become impatient with the process of getting to the end result. Their interest lies in the result, not in how they got there. So while men often naturally relate to goal setting, women just as often resist it because of the focus on the end product rather than on the process.

The challenge for men and women working together on establishing and working toward goals is to reconcile these differing approaches. Men in this situation would do well to see how much enjoyment they can derive from the process of reaching the objective. Female partners can challenge their creativity by helping their mate have fun with the process while developing their own interest in the end result. Two men working together may find themselves so intent on the product that they forget that getting there is just as important, especially to nurturing mutuality in the relationship. Two women may want to avoid this topic altogether. If you're feeling this way, we urge you to look for the fun, intellectual stimulation, adventure, and closeness that can arise from mutually pursuing those steps that will move you closer to living your shared vision.

No one wants to be a slave to goals, driven to accomplish one then another. The approach we want to encourage is one of designing and experiencing the steps you want to take that will move you toward your shared vision. We believe that this is the best way to get there from here.

SOME MISCONCEPTIONS

Having no vision from which to derive goals is a common error when people are goal setting, but there are others. With this in mind, we want to provide some guidelines that will help ensure your success. First, goals ought to be measurable. Otherwise, you will never know when you have reached them. This criterion seems obvious, but many people set goals that are too vague. For instance, deciding on a goal of having enough money to feel comfortable or having sufficient funds for a great vacation each year leaves you with an ideal that is impossible to reach. It cannot be measured—How much is enough? What constitutes a great vacation?—therefore it will never be reached. Make certain your objectives are concrete enough so that you will both know when you have accomplished them.

Second, goals ought to be organic, never carved in stone. We need to be flexible when approaching goals so that if something better happens along the way, and fortunately this often occurs, we can make the appropriate adjustment. The danger of having our noses too close to the grindstone is that we miss new developments, alterations, and shifts that may require that our objectives also be adjusted. We're not suggesting that goals ought to be dumped as soon as something changes, but they do need to be reevaluated from time to time to make sure that they are still worth pursuing and that they will keep you moving in the direction you want. Just as your vision will grow and change as you and your partner do, so, too, will your goals shift in response.

Finally, goals must be attainable. This also seems obvious, but many people set unrealistically high goals or expect themselves to accomplish a goal in too little time. Perfectionists are especially vulnerable to the trap of choosing goals in such a way that they are almost impossible to reach. Or, if the perfectionist does achieve the goal, she or he will decide that the goal wasn't high enough, thus dismissing the effort it took to reach the goal and killing any joy of accomplishment. Since perfectionism is so prevalent in this culture, we will devote some space here to addressing how it sabotages effective progress in building a vision.

Oil and Water
We know oil and water don't mix. Well, neither do reaching goals enthusiastically and being a perfectionist. The biggest challenge related to being a perfectionist is first recognizing that you are one! Most perfectionists believe that if only the rest of the world would do things the way they do them, then everything would be, well, perfect. Perfectionism is based on low self-esteem. Individuals addicted to this way of being contrive ways to reinforce their bad feelings about themselves, even though they may appear to have a strong sense of self. Perfectionists spend great chunks of time attending to and polishing details that don't matter to the overall picture. They waste their own time and everyone else's in trying to make

things "just right." The real motivation is one of control and, often, avoidance of change. Perfectionists generally will not move forward with a project until every detail is worked out ahead of time. They put their energy into controlling the outcome before even beginning. If the outcome differs from the firmly predetermined result, it will be seen as a failure because it didn't meet the preset expectation. Never mind that it might be even better than the preconception— perfectionists have no room for unexpected success. With this rigid approach, perfectionists can reinforce their low self-image by telling themselves they are failures because the project failed to have the planned-for result.

This self-sabotaging behavior is also evident when it comes to goal setting. Perfectionists typically set goals that are much too high to be reached, so when they don't do what they set out to do—something that no one could accomplish—they beat themselves up for being inept or inadequate. When they do happen to fulfill a goal, they negate their accomplishment by assuring themselves that obviously the goal wasn't high enough, thereby dismissing their efforts and killing the joy. In order to avoid these self-made traps, some perfectionists will spend so much time getting ready to begin pursuing the goal that it will become meaningless because of the passage of time, or because someone else will step in and do it. Perfectionists don't delegate—no one can do it as well as they can. Or they drive others crazy by telling them how to do every thing.

Perfectionists also seem to lack a genuine ability to accurately estimate how much time a goal will take to be completed. This is another sabotaging technique, but this inability often stays with even the most vigilant recovering perfectionist. We have both told people who earnestly want to rid themselves of their perfectionist baggage that when trying to figure out how much time to devote to some task, they should make their best guess then quadruple it. This technique, as it turns out, gives them a more accurate idea of how long completing a goal ought to take.

So when we say that goals must be attainable, that word means something completely different to perfectionists than it does to everyone else. If either partner belongs to this group, we suggest some rigorous attention to your behaviors associated with goals.

Attempting to adhere to the perfectionist's pattern as it relates to goal setting and self-sabotage will destroy both of your efforts to develop the kind of life or business you have said you want. "Attainable" means that the amount of time given to achieve the goal is adequate and that the goal is not too high—it's a step rather than a leap. Perfectionists have a way of sounding extremely confident when they say they can accomplish something in a given amount of time. If you know that your perfectionist partner is being unrealistic, you can help to educate him or her. Likewise, if the proposed goal seems too big to be manageable, make your partner aware of that, then work together to break it down into smaller steps. Too often, perfectionists don't realize they are demanding too much of themselves and others.

DEVELOPING GOALS

Now we're ready to begin designing the steps you both want to take so that you can start living out your vision. When you developed your vision, we mentioned that you may discover that you are already living parts of it. If this is the case, jot down which aspects fit this description and discuss how you got to this point. Make some notes for yourselves about what you did independently and together. You may have consciously set goals to make it happen or you may have just somehow gotten where you want to be. Even in this latter scenario, people have inevitably taken certain steps to get where they are, so bringing your natural process to light can give you guidance now. Build on what you already do, learn about each other's preferences in setting and reaching goals, and work together to move toward your vision. Ask yourselves and each other, "How can I make this process enjoyable?"

Pick an Area

Looking at your vision, what area or areas would you like to begin moving toward first? If you selected more than one, which of these is the most important? Sometimes you can work on more than one aspect of your vision at a time—one of you might return to college to earn a degree while the other learns more about investing strategies. One business partner might be better at external marketing while the other is better at creating marketing materials. Improved marketing may be the goal, but it is being addressed by each person working in different areas. In both cases, the partners involved will be supporting each other while focusing on the individual strengths that can move both toward the vision. In other words, you may find yourselves working on goals that address differing aspects of your overall plan, or you may find that you are both addressing the same objective. Building a vision usually takes some amount of time, so give yourselves permission at the outset to work in ways that suit you both.

Develop the Steps

Some of you can sit down with your vision, new messages, and partner and begin writing down the steps you need to take to get where you want to go. Great! Start doing that now. Focusing on one aspect of your shared vision, write down what you will need to accomplish in the next month, three months, six months, nine months, and year to realize that piece. These are suggested time periods, since some parts of your vision will take longer than a year to fully realize while others will take less time. Make sure to check the reality of your timetable—can you each readily accomplish the goals within the allocated period? Do the goals you have written down meet the criteria of being measurable and attainable? Are you willing to allow them to be organic?

Other Approaches

This is one approach to designing goals. However, as we have discussed, people have differing yet equally valid approaches to tasks. Here's where the fortune cookie approach of beginning from the end can be helpful. Focusing on one aspect of your vision that you both agree is the top priority right now, assume that you are already there. In the previous chapter when we were discussing ways to implant your vision into your life, we suggested using as many of your senses as you can to make your vision as real as possible. Employing the same approach, give life to the part of your vision that you have chosen to develop right now. In your mind's eye, see yourself and your partner living in the reality of this part of your vision.

Make it vivid and alive by seeing it and feeling it emotionally and kinesthetically in your body, even adding taste and smell. Keep your eyes closed for several minutes as you use your imagination to make this experience seem as real as possible. Then talk with your partner about what this activity was like. Using what your partner says, add to and embellish your own mental picture. The idea is to build on the notion that you have already realized this part of what you want.

Now, ask yourselves the question, "How did we get there from here? What did we do to make this part of our vision into a reality?" Begin writing down your answers to these questions. As with many other aspects of redesigning your messages and your overall relationship with money, using your sense of humor helps in this process. You can be as absurd as you want to be in speculating about how you achieved your vision. Frequently, out of our humorous speculations come excellent practical ideas. Humor stretches our possibilities. Once you've both exhausted your flow of ideas about the possible steps you would take, you're ready to sort out the realistic from the absurd. These are your goals, the things you need to accomplish that will get you where you want to be. Once you have these steps clearly written out, you can prioritize them according to a reasonable timeline.

Using this "backward" approach enables you to create the same list of one-month, three-month, six-month, nine-month, and one-year goals as following the other way we discussed. When you are comfortable with the approach you've taken to develop your goals (or progress steps or whatever you want to call them), then you are more likely to embrace them as guidelines to help you both get to where you want to be. Being invested in your goals is key to following through with them.

MAKING A COMMITMENT

Now you are ready to make a firm commitment to your goals. Start by focusing on your one-month goals. Decide who is going to do what. Discuss what your first step toward realizing the goal will be and when you will take it. Write all of this out in a commitment statement. For instance: "Tomorrow I will spend two hours in the library researching mutual fund investing." Writing it out and telling your partner what you will do helps to create accountability. Here's another hint: To greatly increase your likelihood of succeeding, do something toward your first goal within the next 24 hours. This immediate follow-through is important in establishing momentum and in getting you moving in your chosen direction.

Supporting Each Other

For some of you, completing the steps necessary to achieve your vision is exciting and invigorating. Others may still harbor some reluctance to engage in the activities required to realize your goals; you may carry an underlying concern that they will take over your life. Compassion and kindness for each other need to dominate your actions. We inevitably encounter challenges as we work toward making our vision a reality. Rather than blaming yourself or your partner for having difficulty, examine the steps you have designed to move you forward. They may not be the appropriate steps, or they may be too big and need to be broken down. Revisiting the specifics of the task is far more fruitful than blaming yourself or your partner for not completing something. Blaming stops the process and invites resentment and eventually ends the journey toward the vision.

Keep Talking and Listening

Working in partnership on your goals may mean that at times you are both devoting time and energy to the same step and at other times you may each be engaged in different aspects of the same goal. Naturally, communication is important throughout this process. Keep each other informed of your progress and discuss any challenges. We recommend a weekly meeting of 30 to 60 minutes, scheduled at the same time each week, throughout this process. The purpose of these meetings is to report on what you have done, ask for assistance if needed, reevaluate the appropriateness of your commitment statements, and define your next steps.

Remember that you are not in this by yourself, you have each other throughout this process. Don't let yourself become frustrated with some goal-related task. Discuss what's going on with your partner and ask for insight and suggestions. In this help-seeking discussion, the focus is on moving toward your vision. Resist the temptation to blame yourself or each other if the path gets rocky.

Meg and Buddy's Story

We coached Meg and Buddy through the initial stages of working together on their goals. They had been married a few years, and although owning their own home was something they both said they wanted, they had never developed the discipline or guidelines to achieve that goal. They would start saving money, then find something else to spend it on. They already knew that having their own home was an important part of their vision, and now they were developing the necessary steps toward that major purchase. One of the first steps was to design a budget that included saving money for a down payment. Meg agreed to take on this responsibility, but she got bogged down in several different approaches to budgeting, then felt overwhelmed when she realized how much money they would have to save. Once this happened, she was stumped. After struggling with her dilemma for several days and becoming increasingly frustrated and overwhelmed, she told Buddy how she was feeling. He told us later that his first instinct was to tell her that budgeting was really simple and that she was just letting herself get overwhelmed unnecessarily. Fortunately, he caught himself before saying anything and remembered our advice—when someone becomes stuck during the process of reaching a goal, the problem is either in the goal or the techniques being used. When you have arrived at your goals using the process we have described, the problem is not with the person.

So Buddy focused on the figures Meg was using to calculate needed savings. They explored various options regarding down payments, and her feelings of being overwhelmed subsided. Once that happened, she could work out a budget that was realistic and manageable and that they could both support.

ACCOMPLISHING YOUR GOAL

Our premise here is that because you have each worked through many old and useless messages about money, and because you have put a lot of effort into redesigning your individual and collective relationships with money, when it comes to goals, you are clear about what you want. You will accomplish your vision. You may need to make some shifts in how you get there, but you will do it. So stay away from blaming yourself when your efforts toward a particular goal aren't going as smoothly as you would like. There are many ways to do things, and you and your partner may simply need to explore additional possibilities.

Another technique that is highly effective in helping people follow through with commitments is using your imagination prior to actually beginning the task. The idea (this is going to sound very familiar) is to use as many senses as you can—visual, kinesthetic, auditory, olfactory, gustatory—and imagine yourself taking the first step toward the first goal, then the next step, and so on until you see yourself meeting your initial objective. Imagine as many details as you can, even exploring in your mind's eye different ways to approach reaching your goal. Here's how you can use this technique. After you have defined your first goal, give yourself a few minutes of quiet, uninterrupted time, close your eyes, and imagine yourself doing all the activities you need to do in order to meet your goal. You may discover problems you hadn't anticipated. It's great to be able to deal with anything that might be troublesome before you even get started. Discuss any blocks that may have come up with your partner, so the two of you can generate ways to resolve the concern. Then revisit your mental plan, implementing your solution to the difficulty, and see how it works out.

This technique does a few important things for you. First, you can do some troubleshooting ahead of time that will make your efforts more productive and efficient as you actually work on completing the goal. No one can anticipate every challenge, and this isn't an exercise to iron out every possible difficulty before starting. If you try to do that, you'll never start! You're exploring alternative ways of approaching your efforts to meet the goal and dealing with any obvious concerns that might stop your progress. In addition, doing this imagery exercise—actually seeing yourself going through all the steps necessary to meet your goal—activates your enthusiasm for the activity. People who use this technique are far more likely to finish what they start than people who simply begin a task without the mental preparation. Finally, using imagery in this way helps to jump-start your creative energies so that they are fully available to you throughout this entire journey toward your vision.

CELEBRATE!

Remember to celebrate your success along the way. Too often, people don't congratulate themselves on a job well done until the entire objective is realized. That could take many months or even a year or more. We need regular encouragement and recognition of the small steps taken along the way. Such acknowledgement keeps us motivated, especially when we have to tackle some less-than-enjoyable task. Your weekly meetings offer a perfect opportunity for giving and receiving a pat on the back or a major hug of recognition. At least once a month, do something special to celebrate both of your efforts. This might be breakfast or dinner out, or even an in-home or at-your-business massage for both of you. Do whatever appropriately acknowledges your willingness to stick with your commitment to yourselves and each other and provides incentive for continuing to move toward your vision.

Getting there from here requires some discipline, application of effective techniques in goal setting and goal achieving, and support from each other. A sense of whimsy and curiosity about what this adventure will bring to you and your partner makes this part of your journey together doubly rewarding.

MOVING FORWARD ▶▶▶▶▶▶▶▶▷

Getting there from here involves both partners designing and experiencing the process that will move you toward your shared vision. These steps need to be undertaken with a sense of adventure and compassion that will get you through any challenges.

1. Have your new messages and vision where you can refer to them.

2. Remember, goals must be measurable, organic, and attainable.

3. Review the section on perfectionist ("Oil and Water"), if necessary.

4. Looking at your vision, ask yourselves what area or areas you would like to move toward first.

5. Write down what you will need to accomplish in the next month, three months, six months, nine months, and year to realize the chosen area of your vision. Or imagine that you are already living that chosen aspect of your vision. Answer the question, "How did we get here?"

6. Decide who is going to do what, when, to get moving toward your first goal.

7. Maintain your mutual support of each other as you progress toward your goals.

WHAT DO WE WANT TO TEACH THE CHILDREN IN OUR LIVES?

As we develop our own positive messages about money, we have a wonderful opportunity to teach the children in our lives healthy money messages. Oh, it will be challenging. There are many competing messages pulling young people down unhealthy paths. Our world has become increasingly commercialized and materialistic. Advertisers are targeting children at younger ages each year, luring them into the world of consumerism with promises and products. Children have more money than we did when we were young. A recent survey of American teens found that about half of them receive an allowance of about $50 each week from their parents. And they spend it with ease, it seems. One study estimated that American teenagers pump more than one billion dollars into the economy each week![1] These figures may come as a surprise to some of us. The challenge of helping children to use the money they have wisely and to plan for the future is great. As we develop healthier attitudes ourselves, we are ready to meet this challenge and demonstrate a new way of coping with money issues.

All adults in a child's life can be teachers of this new way of relating to money. You may be an honorary aunt, uncle, or grandparent or related by blood ties. Whatever your relationship to a young person, you can play an important role as an educator, supporter, and role model. It does, indeed, take a village to raise a child. It also takes a village to teach new, healthy attitudes toward money. Here are some of the ways you can be a good teacher.

CHALLENGING FAMILY MESSAGES

One critical place to start teaching children about money is at the level of our own family money messages. We know that we cannot teach others to be healthy if we are not healthy ourselves. And since most children seem to have built-in hypocrisy detectors, we know it would be futile to try. The old saying, updated, is true—"Children do as we do, not as we say." So we must continue to examine our old family messages to be sure that they reflect who we are today. That means looking at the past to pick out messages that still fit and can be used to our benefit. It means replacing old messages that no longer work with those that do. It means continuing to develop our own financial comfort level so that we show our children a new way of being around money. We are no longer bound by the past but are able to find ways that fit who we are today. As we live out our new messages, the information and behaviors are transmitted to the children in our lives.

We also model family messages as couples. Our new attitudes regarding the sharing of responsibilities related to family finances demonstrate to our children a healthier way of being. Our caring, cooperation, and clear, honest communication give our children new examples to follow. They learn that the financial management of the family is the joint responsibility of equal partners.

We also want to be sure that we help our children move beyond the old gender-based limitations. Boys and girls are equally capable of handling money, so we want to give both the opportunities to learn and grow. Both can learn to take care of themselves financially so they don't fall into the old role of needing to rescue or be rescued. Instead of looking for a good provider, girls can learn that they can provide for themselves. Instead of being pushed into the role of being that good provider, boys should understand that they can share responsibilities with a caring partner. We demonstrate this equality and sharing by our behaviors as we live out our new messages.

As we challenge the old messages and replace them with new ones, we can move to a healthier way of being. We no longer have battles about money because we've learned to communicate and cooperate. We continue to rewrite the old messages, replacing them with clear, healthy ones. By including our children in our money-related growth, as much as their ages allow, we lift the secrecy about money. When we involve them in designing a healthy relationship with money, we teach decision making based on self-power. Our children see our progress and grow and progress in this area as well.

CHALLENGING OUR OWN ATTITUDES

One of the most important ways we can teach our children about money is by communicating and demonstrating our own healthy attitudes. We can show our children that we view money as a tool—one that can help us live the kind of life we have envisioned. We can talk about money freely and honestly, and we can share our family goals and visions with our children. We can make sure that money is not a taboo subject in our family, and that it is not used for game playing, power, control, or punishment.

We also need to make sure that our behaviors match our attitudes. In a recent study parents were found to hold one attitude but demonstrate a contradictory behavior. While the parents surveyed by the American Savings Education Council reported that they saw themselves as good financial role models, their behaviors indicated otherwise. More than half of them reported carrying excessive debt on their credit cards and paying high interest rates to do so. Only 45 percent of the parents polled said they made a budget and stuck to it. Further, 58 percent of the parents in the survey were not knowledgeable about where to invest money to receive the highest rates of return.[2] Children are more likely to follow our example than to do what we say. If we truly want to be good role models, we need to get our financial lives in order and live in accordance with our values.

CHALLENGING SOCIETAL MESSAGES

Another important thing we can do for the young people in our lives is to help them develop a healthy skepticism regarding the messages they receive from our consumer-oriented culture. Teaching young people to identify and act from their own values rather than those imposed by society gives them the power of choice. It also gives the self-respect that comes from learning to make appropriate choices.

The Pull of Advertising

We live in a society in which the typical child views 20,000 television ads each year. Given this constant barrage of advertising, it's no wonder our children have become increasingly materialistic. They are told that in order to be considered worthwhile, they have to own a particular brand or wear a certain style. The push to buy and spend surrounds our young people. To help them become more thoughtful consumers, we need to teach them that they can make choices and not to be blindly pushed by the pressure of advertisers.

We can help our children become better consumers by teaching them to separate their self-esteem from their possessions. We must help them understand that, contrary to what the advertising constantly surrounding them says, buying a certain product will not add to their worth or popularity. Children need to know that their worth does not depend on what they have but who they are. True self-esteem comes from within. It is based on capability and accomplishment, not on the amount of material goods we possess. If we can help our children understand this, and give them ways they can achieve and feel good about themselves, they are better equipped to withstand the constant barrage of advertising that pushes them to purchase, possess, and consume.

Helping Adolescents Make Conscious Choices

As we watch the young people in our lives struggle to establish their independence, we are presented with a marvelous opportunity. Most teens fail to see the supreme irony of their adolescent years. In spite of their vehement insistence that "nobody can tell me what to do," teens are, in truth, highly controlled by the push of advertising and the pressure of peers. Our task as adults is to gently guide them to the understanding that true independence comes from critical evaluation of the messages surrounding them. We can help them to analyze media messages by teaching them to dissect advertisements. Teens can learn to look beneath the glitzy persuasion to the real message. Asking such questions as: "What is the appeal of this advertisement?" "How is the appeal made?" "What does this mean to me?" "Do I believe it?" will help teens appraise the promises of advertisers. Once they can critically evaluate the messages they receive from the media, they can then make judgments about what they really want.

Wants Versus Needs

We also can help our children learn to distinguish between a want and a need. This is critical to breaking the hold of excess consumerism. Most of us would define a need as something essential to our survival. How much of what we see in advertising really qualifies as a need, using this definition? We can teach our children to make good decisions by doing a brief economic analysis. We can teach them to ask: "Do I really need this item or do I merely want it? If I really want it, how much is it worth to me? Three hours of work time, four? Is it worth spending my allowance on this? How much use will I get out of it? Is this really where I want to spend my money?" Note also that these questions are meant to be analytical, not judgmental. This kind of critical thinking helps children evaluate how important an item is to them and gives them the choice of whether or not to buy it. Since adults are not immune to the constant push to buy and spend, we need to do the same kind of questioning. So we teach by example, as well as words, that possessions are not the most important thing in life. This is a healthier way to approach buying, by making it a conscious choice. Giving our children the power of choice is excellent training for spending and for life.

STEPS TO TAKE NOW

In our workshops, we are frequently asked about the best time to begin teaching children about money. Our response is always the same: begin now. Whatever the age of the child, you can find appropriate ways to teach the lessons needed. Here are some steps to begin.

Step One—The Opportunity to Handle Money

In order for children to learn how to deal with money, they need to have experience doing so. This experience should start as soon as children are able to understand what money is all about. An allowance can be an excellent way to give children the opportunity to possess funds of their own and to learn to manage them. Parents can set up some guidelines, using a combination of structure and flexibility, to help children learn principles of both saving and spending. Some families, for example, have a rule that a certain percentage of the allowance goes into long-term saving, and a certain percentage is saved for gifts and other special-occasion items. In addition, some of the allowance is earmarked for day-to-day expenses. The remainder can be spent as the child sees fit. Children need to make mistakes with money in order to learn what not to do. So, as difficult as it may be, the parent stays out of this part of the financial education. If money is blown on a trip to the video arcade or a toy that breaks after one use, the parents allows the experience to be the teacher. If we can resist rescuing, or conversely, judging and shaming, our children will learn quickly to be careful spenders.

Step Two—Learning How to Save and Invest

Children can have saving accounts as soon as they are old enough to understand the concept. They can share in the experience of opening an account and adding to it at regular intervals.

The power of investing is another important aspect of money that children need to be taught. They can be given small amounts to invest so that they can discover where and how to invest money. Parents and other adults can provide guidance, but your children will surprise you with how quickly they learn the basic principles of investing, and how eagerly they look forward to checking on their accounts.

Special occasions provide wonderful opportunities to help children learn about saving and investing. Adults can give a monetary gift that is specifically earmarked for the sole purpose of investing. We know of one family friend who gave two teenagers a sum of money with the stipulation that they invest it in mutual funds. After an initial bout of grumbling about what a "boring" gift this was, the young people set about using the money given them. They studied mutual funds and picked a place to invest. As they watched the funds grow, their experience was enough to turn them into confirmed investors. They broadened their knowledge and were pleased with the results.

Step Three—Participation in Family Financial Matters
Wise parents get their children involved in family financial matters by including them in discussions about the budget and other issues. In this way, parents send a message that dealing with money is a routine part of life and something children can and should do. Children, in turn learn to feel comfortable and confident about their ability to handle money. Both parents and children benefit by this cooperative effort.

The Family Budget   Children should be included in discussions that have to do with the family budget. Knowing how much the family has to spend on groceries and helping to spend it, for example, may head off fights at the grocery store when the child begs to buy something that is not in the budget. Children can also learn to comparison shop and begin to see that not all purchases yield equal value for the money.

One mother we know used a grocery-store expedition to teach her children how to shop wisely. Since they knew they only had a certain amount of their grocery budget to spend in the produce section, she let her children decide whether they wanted a small container of blueberries, which were out of season, or a large bag of apples, which were in season. The children wisely thought it over and decided they would rather have the larger quantity of apples. Their mother was secretly relieved by their choice, but she was also willing to allow them to learn a different lesson if they had chosen the blueberries. "It takes more time to shop sometimes," she told us. "But I think the lessons they are learning are worth the time involved. I want them to be able to make wise decisions on their own and this is one way to help them do that."

Children can participate in major family expenditures as well as routine shopping expeditions. Of course we aren't saying your children should decide which new car you will purchase. They can, however, be included in discussions that will teach valuable lessons about how to investigate and select big-ticket items. Children can learn about sticker price, depreciation, maintenance, insurance, and other considerations that go into a major purchase. They can begin to learn about making wise decisions, getting a good buy, and avoiding the impulse-buying trap. Seeing you plan for both routine and major purchases gives children the message that family finances are a part of family life, and that responsible spending takes thought, consideration, and planning on the part of all family members. The rewards of this approach are increased self-esteem and the feeling of accomplishment that comes from making wise decisions.

Handling Setbacks   Part of including children in family financial discussions is being honest about setbacks in the family situation. Children who feel secure are amazingly resilient. If a parent is laid off, they can absorb this information without being made fearful. Likewise, if a downturn in the stock market means that there is less disposable income, children can be told this as well. Children are going to be affected by changes in the family's situation. They will sense their parents' stress even if they aren't told specific details. And sometimes what children imagine and worry about is far worse than the reality of the situation. Being honest with our children is a better strategy than sugarcoating the truth or withholding information.

If we want our children to be comfortable with money, they need to know that we trust them to handle the bad news as well as the good. If children see the change as something the family is handling together, they will feel safe and confident. When they see the change as something that cannot be discussed, they will be fearful. How much they are told depends, of course, on the age of the children. This is the case with any information we give to children, whether we are explaining the death of a loved pet or discussing the loss of a job. Since children take their cues from the adults in their lives, we have the ability to help them see change as a challenge or a tragedy. If it is presented as a challenge, most parents are pleasantly surprised at how well children can handle a change in family finances. They naturally want to help, and they will respond to an invitation, rather than a demand, to contribute to the family's well-being.

Step Four—Acquiring Lifelong Money Values
A study conducted at Iowa State University found that college students who had healthy attitudes about money learned them at a young age. These students had parents who expressed confidence in

their abilities. Further, their parents guided the students to develop a value system related to money by helping them formulate goals for saving.[3]

You can do the same with your children by acting in ways that demonstrate your belief that it is important to spend less than you earn. As your children watch you put money away for their college educations, they learn that this is how families work toward financial goals. When you discuss family financial goals with your children, they will learn from those discussions. If your children see you act in accordance with sound money values, they will learn to do the same.

Adults also have the chance to set a good example for children by acting with integrity and fair play in all their financial dealings. Teaching children to be honest in all things conveys a valuable life lesson. Taking time to return the excess change given in error by the check-out clerk at your neighborhood convenience store sets an example of honesty. Allowing children to see you put in a full day's work for the salary you receive shows them that you value fair play. If you live according to your beliefs, children are likely to follow what they see and accept it as a way of life.

Step Five—The Opportunity to Discuss Money

The days of keeping secrets are over. As parents, you can involve your children in ongoing discussions about money and its role in your lives. In that way you will demystify the subject, so that your children talk easily and freely about it. You can bring educational materials home to teach your children how money works. The media can be incorporated as a tool; you can teach children how to find financial information in newspapers, on television, and in magazines and books. Perhaps you will start a family investment club or you will encourage your children to find one at school. A matter-of-fact approach makes the formerly taboo topic of money a comfortable part of your daily lives. As a result, your children will be comfortable and knowledgeable about money and its purpose.

Step Six—Money Serving a Higher Purpose

Children can learn about giving to others from watching the adults in their lives demonstrate this behavior. Adults who live out their values by giving time or money to causes that contribute to the greater good show children how to make a difference in the world. Even the youngest child can understand the importance of sharing what they have with others. And this sharing teaches the lesson that money can be used for more than just possessions. The spiritual aspect of money is especially apparent when it is used for a higher purpose.

Teaching the children in our lives about money requires ongoing awareness of our own issues. As we abandon our old, unhealthy messages, we allow our children to do so as well. Our attitudes toward our own money issues will demonstrate to our children that being in charge of our own lives is the way to live. As we encourage the children in our lives to meet the challenge of developing a healthy relationship with money, we continue to grow as well. We have the opportunity to serve as role models to the new generation—an awesome responsibility and an exciting challenge.

MOVING FORWARD ▶▶▶▶▶▶▶▶▶

One of the most important tasks we face as adults is that of guiding young people toward a healthy relationship with money. In order to do this, we need to have our own issues under control so we can be effective role models. This chapter offers suggestions for fostering positive attitudes and behaviors in the lives of our children. Here are some steps you can take to achieve this goal.

1. List eight to ten of the most important money *facts* you want to convey to the young people in your life.

2. List three to five of the most important money *values* you want to convey to the young people in your life.

3. Prioritize both lists, moving from most important to least important.

4. Using your prioritized lists of facts and values, write an action plan detailing how you will go about passing on this information.

5. Commit to have your first money discussion with the young person(s) in your life. Be aware of any discomfort this creates for you.

6. Do a check of your own money attitudes. Identify any areas you feel need continued attention. Make an appointment with yourself to work on this issue.

16

LIVING POSITIVELY: SHARING AND GROWING AS COUPLES

Let's face it. Growing together as a couple isn't easy, whether you're building a life or a business together. Getting two people with different backgrounds, life experiences, values, and hopes together almost guarantees difficulties. There are days when you feel like running for the nearest exit. There are also days when you sincerely believe you are incredibly lucky to be with this particular person. Learning to be with another person in an intimate relationship has the potential to be one of the most satisfying things you can do. And it is one of the greatest challenges you will face in your life.

Redesigning your relationship with money is an equally formidable task, with a similar potential for reaping great benefits. So working on money and relationship issues at the same time is quite a challenge. Meeting this challenge requires a lot of effort and tenacity. Part of the hard work is changing some of your old beliefs and behaviors. We recognize that change is difficult—there is no doubt about it. Human beings cling to the familiar even when it isn't necessarily in our best interest. The old saying about the devil you know being preferable to the devil that you don't know fits for most of us. In this book, we have asked you to give up the known and embrace the unfamiliar. And you have been willing to do so. Good for you! You are to be commended for the time and effort you both have invested in redesigning your relationship with money as a couple. Having come this far, it is important to consider what you can do to maintain your growth and continue your progress into the future.

LOOKING AT WHAT YOU HAVE LEARNED

Learning is more powerful when we do something to incorporate it into our daily lives. Doing so gives us the opportunity to summarize what we know so far and to set goals for future growth. With this in mind, we ask you to take a minute to think about the chapters in the book, reflect on what you have learned, and reaffirm your goals for the future.

Part One—Messages from the Past

As you worked your way through this book, we have asked you to look at messages from the past that may still be operating in the present. You constructed your genogram to identify family money attitudes. You also looked at cultural messages to see if any of these affect your current beliefs and behaviors. Take a minute to review the messages that you are ready to leave behind. List them here:

Family messages I wish to change:

Family messages I wish to keep:

Cultural messages I wish to change:

Cultural messages I wish to keep:

Part Two—Messages from the Present

We also asked you to look at your present money issues. While not all the areas we discussed will be relevant to you, it is helpful to take another look at what you have learned and to identify any potentially challenging areas.

Money and Self-Worth Concerning money and self-worth I learned that:

I still want to grow in the following area(s):

We as a couple will grow by:

Money and Emotions Concerning money and emotions I learned that:

I still want to grow in the following area(s):

We as a couple will grow by:

Money Values   Concerning money values I learned that:

I still want to grow in the following area(s):

We as a couple will grow by:

Money and Secrecy   Concerning money and secrecy I learned that:

I still want to grow in the following area(s):

We as a couple will grow by:

The Power Differential   Concerning money and power I learned that:

I still want to grow in the following area(s):

We as a couple will grow by:

Love, Sex, and Money   Concerning money and sex I learned that:

I still want to grow in the following area(s):

We as a couple will grow by:

Part Three—Making Plans: Developing a Couple's Vision of Money

This section asked you to look at some ways to keep a clear focus as you worked to redesign your relationship with money. Let's look at some of the strengths you possess as well as some of the areas you have earmarked for change.

Couples Communication

Strengths we now possess in communicating as a couple:

Areas we would like to grow:

Writing New Messages

Positive money messages we have now are:

New money messages we want to incorporate into our lives are:

Developing a New Vision

Our new vision of money is:

Getting There from Here

Strengths we currently possess:

Couple goals we have identified are:

Steps we will take to achieve these goals are:

We recommend that you use this format to assess your growth periodically. Once you have completed the initial assessment, you will find you can move through your update rapidly. The progress you see will encourage you to continue to revise old messages. You will also be more aware of areas you want to pinpoint for continued development as you design new goals.

MAINTAINING YOUR GROWTH

Staying healthy in an unhealthy world is another challenge you face. Sometimes it seems that there isn't a lot of support for being a couple. We even have television shows like *Temptation Island,* where the goal is to pull couples apart! We talk about family values, but we frequently fail to give couples the support they need to strengthen their relationships. In spite of the fact that the average marriage has a 50-percent chance of survival, many managed care companies won't pay for couples counseling. And we rarely provide same-sex couples with the recognition and financial benefits that would assist them in maintaining their partnership. So we talk about wanting to strengthen families but we rarely take any concrete action to do so.

As a society, our attitudes about money also need some serious revision. We are pushed and pulled by the forces of materialism.

The United States has more shopping malls than high schools, according to a recent *Newsweek* article.[1] We are encouraged to buy and consume to an ever-increasing degree.

Money continues to be misused in our society. People try to wield it as a source of power and influence. Secrecy and misplaced priorities surround it. We are frequently insecure about our ability to earn and manage it.

Having a good relationship and a healthy attitude toward money can be difficult. That's the bad news. The good news is that you, as a couple, have the power to write your own messages and set your own terms. You *can* have a healthy relationship with each other and with money. You already know that, or you wouldn't be reading this book. Working through the exercises in this book is an excellent start. It affirms your commitment to each other and encourages your growth as a couple. Here are some suggestions to help you maintain that growth and to build on it.

1. **Know what you are arguing about.** Having come this far in the book, you are aware that fights about money are usually about something else. Hopefully, you have begun to identify your triggers related to this issue. Now your task is to distinguish underlying issues from surface issues. If you are fighting about exceeding the limit on the charge card, we encourage you to find out if there are underlying problems that you need to deal with before you are ready to handle the charge card overdraft. Are you really fighting about power? Anger? Feelings of being left out? What is really happening here? If you take time to identify the underlying issue, you will find the clarity and direction that will allow you to get to the heart of the matter quickly, deal with it, and move on.

2. **Develop some couples rituals involving money to keep you on track.** As mentioned earlier, you might want to go over the couples and money assessment in this book on a regular basis. The process of articulating and evaluating your goals will keep you focused and on target. Other rituals work as well. One couple sets aside time every six weeks to review their financial

plan and see how close they are to achieving the goals they set for themselves. Another couple we know takes time at the end of the month to review their household spending. They have a small celebration each time they are able to add extra funds to their savings account. Finding rituals you can share as a couple reinforces the idea that your money, like your life, is a shared partnership.

3. **Spend time with like-minded couples.** You will want to find couples who have similar values and goals as yours. That will make it easier for you to affirm your own values and stick with them. If all your friends insist on owning the latest and the best, the task of honoring your own values as they relate to spending will be more difficult. If the couples you socialize with aren't committed to making their relationships stronger, it will be more difficult for you to do so. Are we suggesting you only mix with couples exactly like you? Certainly not. Diversity is enriching and enjoyable. You will want to know a variety of different people for your growth and development. We are suggesting that you find a core group of couples who share most of your values. With their support, you will find it easier to stay focused on what is important to you. And the company you keep will reinforce your values.

   If you are in a business partnership, join business organizations that draw the kinds of entrepreneurs who share a similar philosophy. Networking with these business owners can help you both to re-energize for success.

4. **Make a commitment to continue to strengthen your bond with each other and to clarify your relationship with money.** By now you are aware that both issues are difficult and both require work. Know that you will have good and bad days together. All couples do. Commit to riding out the bad times as you work to find your way back to the good ones. Do the work that is necessary to move your relationship to a place of growth and well-being.

5. **Value cooperation over competition.** Cooperation means that you are both working toward joint goals, while competition

implies winners and losers. When you cooperate, you are saying that having a successful relationship is more important than being "right." Thinking from the viewpoint of a couple requires that you put the well-being of the relationship above your own. That doesn't mean we are asking you to lose your identity in the relationship. We *are* suggesting that if your relationship is important to you, you should begin to think in terms of "What is best for us?" and "What will move our company/relationship forward?" rather than "What is best for me?"

6. **Acknowledge your uniqueness as a couple.** You will design couples rituals and ways of dealing with money issues that work for you. Have confidence in your ability to forge your own path, even when your family and friends do things differently. You have the right to set your own terms and find ways that strengthen you as a couple. In a business, what enhances you as partners improves your organization.

7. **Take time to celebrate the positive changes you are making.** As you become more comfortable with your money issues, you will start to notice changes. You may find that you are discussing money without the old rancor. Supportive listening skills and problem-solving skills mark your conversations. The old issues that were such sticking points are becoming more manageable. Your feelings toward each other are warmer and more positive. This is the time to celebrate your changes by taking some couple time to do something you both enjoy. What you do will depend on you and your budget. You can pick an extravagant celebration or one that is less so. Setting aside time to celebrate the changes you have forged allows you to accomplish two important objectives. You acknowledge the efforts you have made so far and you further strengthen your relationship as a couple. Both are worth celebrating!

A FINAL WORD

Looking at your couple dynamics and redesigning your relationship to money is challenging. It may even be frustrating and painful at times. We encourage you to stick with it. Our work with couples tells us that the rewards are worth the effort. We have seen couples make powerful changes as they redesign their relationship with money and with each other. Their bonds became closer and they moved toward their goals with increased clarity and cooperation. You can do the same. We wish you success as you continue the journey toward a new relationship with money.

NOTES

Chapter 4

1. Lisa Sheppard, "Couples Disagree on Money Management Matters," *ACES News*, University of Illinois, April 6, 2000, p. 1. http://www.ag.uiuc.edu/news/articles/955031482.html.

2. "Are Men More Insecure With Mates Who Earn More Money?" *Jet*, April 10, 2000, p.1. http://www.findarticles.com/cf__0/m1355/18__97/61573827/print.jhtml.

3. Ibid., p. 1.

4. Galina Espinoza, "Who's the Money Boss?" *Working Mother*, February 1999, p. 17.

5. Jay MacDonald, "Gender Spender: Sex Sets Your Money DNA,"*Bankrate.com*, July 22, 2001, p. 2. http://www.bankrate.com/brm/news/sav/20000620.asp.

6. Ibid., p. 3.

7. Ibid., p. 4.

8. Ibid., p. 3.

9. "National Survey Finds: Financially Speaking, Many Single Young Women Show Signs of 'Carrie Bradshaw Syndrome,' " *Oppenheimer Funds, Inc.*, May 1, 2001, p. 3. http://biz.yahoo.com/prnews/010501/nytu080.html.

10. Mary Rowland, "Investment Clubs Show That Gender Doesn't Matter," *Ameritrade*, p. 1. http://moneycentral.msn.com/articles/invest/basics/1291.asp.

11. Betty Carter, "Love, Honor and Negotiate," *Psychology Today*, November/December 1997, p. 84.

12. John W. Santrock, *Psychology* (Boston: McGraw-Hill Higher Education, 2000), p. 579.

Chapter 5

1. Linda Brannon, *Gender-Psychological Perspectives* (Boston: Allyn and Bacon, 1999), p. 227.

2. Ibid., p. 229.

3. Ibid., p. 233.

4. Frank Swertlow, "Money Isn't the Only Thing of Value Lost in Volatile

Times," *Los Angeles Business Journal,* May 22, 2000, http://www.find articles.com/cf__0m5072/21__22/62534770/print.jhtml.

5. M.D. Newcomb and J. Rabow, "Gender, Socialization and Money," *Journal of Applied Social Psychology,* v. 29, n. 4, 1999, p. 870.

6. Ibid.

7. Mary Rowland, "The Basics—Why Some People Get Into Trouble with Debt," *MSN Money Central,* http://www.moneycentral.msn.com/arti cles/banking/saving.

8. "Many Women on Welfare Have Sex-Abuse History," *The Arizona Daily Star,* November 28, 1999, p. 4A.

9. Ibid.

10. Bruce Shenitz, "Out of Balance (Gay Couples Where One Partner Earns More Than the Other)," http://www.findarticles.com/cf__0/m1589/ 1999__April__27/54492595/pl/article.jhtml.

11. Jay MacDonald, "Gender Spender," p. 3.

12. "National Survey Finds."

13. MacDonald, p. 4.

Chapter 8

1. Michelle Singletary, "That Little White Lie about That Little Black Dress Can Lead to a Big Fight about Finances," *The Washington Post,* July 29, 2001, p. H01.

2. Cloé Madanes with Claudio Madanes, *The Secret Meaning of Money* (San Francisco, Jossey-Bass, 1994), p. 79.

3. Bob Anez, "Charles Kuralt's Secret Life," *Salon.com,* June 8, 1999, http://salon.com/people/feature/1999/06/08/kuralt.

Chapter 9

1. Patricia Evans. *The Verbally Abusive Relationship.* Adams Media Corporation, Holbrook, MA, 1996.

2. Susan Campbell, Ph.D. *The Couple's Journey: Intimacy as a Path to Wholeness.* Impact Publishers, San Luis Obispo, CA., 1983.

Chapter 10

1. *All Things Considered,* National Public Radio, August 14, 2001, http://npr.com.

2. Melissa Burdic Harmon, "The Tragedy of Doris Duke—All the Money in the World Couldn't Buy Her Happiness," *Biography*, November 2001, p. 104.

3. Coral Amende, *Hollywood Confidential* (New York: Penguin Books, 1997), p. 187.

4. Interview with Hugh Hefner, *Fresh Air with Terry Gross*, National Public Radio, November 29, 1999, http://www.npr.com.

5. Amende, p. 213.

6. Amende, p. 216.

7. Marcia Millman, *Warm Hearts and Cold Cash* (New York: The Free Press, 1991), p. 5.

8. Michael Reynard, *Money Secrets of the Rich and Famous* (New York: Allworth Press, 1999), p. 71.

9. Millman, p. 5.

10. "Men, Women, and Presents—Likes and Dislikes," *USA Today*, December 1998, p. 2. http://findarticles.com.cf—0/m1272/2643—127/53390136/print.jhtml.

11. Susan Crain Bakos, "Explosive Sex: The Surprising Turn-On You Can't Ignore," *Redbook*, August 2001, p. 103.

12. Amende, p. 171

13. Leslie McRay with Ted Schwarz, *Kept Women—Confessions from a Life of Luxury* (New York: William Morrow & Company, 1990), p. 36.

14. *Men, Sex, and Rape* (Oak Forest, IL: MPI Home Video, 1992).

15. Amende, p. 198.

16. Amende, p. 198.

17. Amende, p. 198.

Chapter 11

1. Julie C. Aniol and Douglas K. Snyder, "Differential Assessment of Financial and Relationship Distress: Implications for Couples Therapy," *Journal of Marital and Family Therapy*, July 1997, v. 23, n. 3, p. 348.

2. "Practice Issues: A Selection of Couples Education Programs," *Psychotherapy Finances*, July 1999, p. 8.

Chapter 15

1. "Teens and Money," *Brown University Child and Adolescent Behavior Newsletter*, April 2000, p. 1. http://www.findarticles.com/cf—0/mo537/4—16/61791013/print.jhtml.

2. Humberto Cruz, "Parents Should Teach Financial Wisdom to Children," *Houston Chronicle.com,* http://houston.webpoint.com/finance/mm20010430.html.

3. Rowland, Why Some People Get into Trouble with Debt, p. 3.

Chapter 16

1. Anna Quindlen, "Honestly—You Shouldn't Have," *Newsweek,* Dec. 3, 2001, p. 76.

●INDEX